# Early Onset Blog

## The Friendship Connection
## and
## Other Essays

From: earlyonset.blogspot.com

By

## L. S. Fisher

M**O**ZARK

*www.MozarkPress.com*

Published by Mozark Press, www.Mozarkpress.com
PO Box 1746, Sedalia, MO 65302


**Cover Picture: Whitney and Mariah at the Memory Walk**

**Acknowledgement: Cover design and book layout by H. Ream**

**DISCLAIMER:** Statements or opinions expressed in the stories and articles of this publication are those of the author and do not necessarily represent the views or positions of any person or entity associated with publication of the book or the Alzheimer's Association.

ISBN: **978-0-9844385-0-1**

# Dedication

The Early Onset Alzheimer's Blog is dedicated to Jimmy D. Fisher and to all whose lives have been changed by a debilitating disease and to their families.

Other Titles

By

L. S. Fisher

Alzheimer's Anthology of
Unconditional Love

Early Onset Blog
Essays from an Online Journal

Available at www.lsfisher.com

# Table of Contents

Introduction.............................................................7
Un-Deck the Halls ...................................................9
I Am an Ambassador! ...........................................12
Airplane Crash Survivors .....................................15
Will Work for Food ...............................................18
It's a Small World..................................................21
Do You Think You Can, or Think You Can't? .....24
Love is Never Out of Style....................................27
Health Fairs Make Me Sick! ................................29
Snow Isn't as Much Fun as It Used to Be............33
Reality TV: The Final Rose—or Not ...................36
Missouri Advocates at State Capitol
        for Memory Day...........................................39
What Would Jim Do? ...........................................42
Purple Passion for Alzheimer's
        at the Public Policy Forum..........................44
Clown Noses, Laughter and Tears .......................48
Teddy Bear Smiles and Not So Sweet Dreams.......51
Memories of a Rocky Mountain Morning.............54
Stand Up and Be Counted....................................57
The Over-Fifty Diagnostic Test ...........................60
When Pigs Fly: Swine Flu Immunization..............64
Lessons Learned from Scott the Piano Guy ..........67
Honor our Everyday Heroes.................................70
The Alzheimer's Project........................................73
Wild Turkey Alarm Clock ...................................77
Murphy's Week .....................................................80
He Wouldn't Harm a Fly ......................................84
Home Videos: I Cried Until I Laughed.................87
Music Therapy Stimulates Memories ...................90
Thinking with My Heart .......................................93

Life is Good.................................................. 95
Living Words: Therapeutic Writing
    for Early-Stage Dementia.................................. 98
Compassionate Allowances ........................... 101
Hurry Up Patience! .................................... 104
Country Living—Not Just for Farmers ............. 107
Not So Friendly Competition ......................... 110
Vacation—Recharging Batteries ...................... 114
Ted and Norma: Promises to Keep.................... 117
If I Make it through September! ...................... 119
White Rabbit Syndrome: Always Late ............... 121
The Friendship Connection............................ 124
Put My House in Order ................................. 127
Autumn: Trick or Treat ................................ 130
Auto Tool Kit: AAA and a Cell Phone.............. 133
In Touch with the Season: Scary Reading........... 137
In a Perfect World...................................... 141
Fall Back: An Extra Hour.............................. 145
Turtles, Tunnels, and Denial........................... 148
Hugs Are Better Than Drugs ......................... 151
Everything Changes..................................... 155
Let it Glow .............................................. 158
Widows Don't Wear Black............................. 161
Alzheimer's Support Group: HBO Screening..... 164
Sparkle Bright with Fairy Dust ....................... 168
Wrap It Up............................................... 171

# Introduction

We never know when life is going to take a detour and veer away from our well-laid plans. My detour began about fifteen years ago on a day that began like any other. I had no foreboding that two routine questions would close the door on the life that was and throw open a gaping hole for the life to be.

My husband, Jim, and I were at a dealership to sign loan papers. During the course of signing the documents, Jim couldn't remember his social security number. His social had been his service number and I was surprised, but not alarmed, that he couldn't come up with it. I rattled off his number from memory.

If that had been the only sign, I would have dismissed it. The next question was, "What is your birth date?" When Jim didn't know the answer to that question, I knew the problem was bigger than a momentary memory lapse.

Jim was forty-nine years old, and the eventual diagnosis of an Alzheimer's type of dementia was a shock to both of us. At the time, neither of us knew much about Alzheimer's. We quickly learned Alzheimer's isn't a joke about people losing their memory; it is an incurable disease that causes brain cell death.

I began a quest to learn everything possible about dementia and read every scrap of material I could find about Alzheimer's. I badgered Alzheimer's staff and other Alzheimer's caregivers. I spent countless hours searching Internet health sites. I posted to forums and cast a wide net to haul in information. I wanted to know what lay ahead and how to handle it.

After Jim's death in 2005, I began a blog dedicated to his memory and to reach out to others facing Alzheimer's. Because I know the importance of humor, I don't always write serious essays.

The word used most often to describe the early onset blog is "unusual." The blog is not only dedicated to early-onset dementia, it is dedicated to living life to the fullest and finding humor in everyday life.

If you think it is more important to count blessings than to curse fate, you should enjoy *Early Onset Blog: The Friendship Connection and Other Essays.*

# Un-Deck the Halls
## Saturday, January 3, 2009

Well, here it is, the first Saturday in January, and I haven't taken down my Christmas decorations. The worse part about putting it off, we have been blessed with sunshine and 70 degree weather today.

One thing I've learned, after living my entire life in Missouri, is how unpredictable the weather can be. I walked outside earlier to check my mail and wore a short sleeved T-shirt. Two weeks ago, we had an artic blast that left our water frozen, and I went outside wearing my insulated coveralls, a heavy coat, and a stocking cap pulled low on my forehead. I looked and felt like the little boy in *Christmas Story* who couldn't bend his arms or legs once he donned his snowsuit.

Thawing frozen pipes used to be Jim's job. Then, after dementia limited Jim's abilities, the responsibility shifted to my shoulders. Several years ago on a cold winter night, his mom called me to tell me our water had frozen. We shared a well and it was behind her house next door. Jim sat in front of the TV watching *Walker Texas Ranger* and didn't even look at me when I told him the news. I put on a pair of Jim's coveralls and called my son, Eric, and brother-in-law. By the time I got decked out in my warm clothes, the two of them were assessing the situation.

"Your dad didn't even care that the water was frozen," I told my son. "He's still at home watching TV."

"I bet he would have cared if the electricity went out and he couldn't watch *Walker*," Eric said.

There is no such thing as typical weather in Missouri. You just take it as it comes and deal with it.

For some reason, I thought that once the holidays were over, I could relax for a while. Ha! The next few months are going to be busier than ever. Today, I need to un-deck the halls and prepare for two upcoming meetings—one tomorrow and one on Thursday. So, I've just been flitting back and forth between reports, emails, laundry, taking down decorations, and thinking that I would really like to go out on the deck, put my feet up and watch the birds.

It's foolish to waste a spring day in the dead of winter, and I do need to take the Christmas lights off the deck railing. After all, by next Saturday the lights may be covered with a coat of ice. Subzero wind chills might make me want to burrow into a blanket and watch an *NCIS* marathon.

My granddaughter will be here soon and if I don't get the halls un-decked, she will no doubt tell me, "Grandma Linda, Christmas is *over*."

I have the Christmas tree put away, but still have a few hours work ahead of me. I can't decide if the chirping birds outside my window are urging me to hurry up and finish, or just put it off until another day.

# I Am an Ambassador!
## Saturday, January 10, 2009

Yesterday was an exasperating day at work—one of those days when Murphy's Law was king and lord of my office. Phone interruptions broke my concentration and had begun to really annoy me. It seemed everybody had a problem and dog-gone-it I had enough of my own!

When one more call came in, I forced my voice to a calmness I no longer felt. This call, instead of adding to my angst, lifted my spirits. Ashley Burden from the Mid-Missouri Chapter called to ask if I would be the Alzheimer's Association Ambassador for Pettis County.

"Sure," I said. "What will I be doing? Do I need to know a foreign language?"

"No foreign language required. And you will pretty much be doing what you already do," she said. "As ambassador, you will speak to civic organizations—you know, give the fifteen minute spiel on the services provided by the Chapter."

"I know a lot of fifteen minute spiels," I admitted. I learned the fifteen minute spiels years ago when I was Memory Walk Coordinator and I haven't shut up since.

During the course of our conversation, Ashley also told me about a new program called LEARN to address early stage problems. This exciting program funded by a Missouri Grant will provide additional guidance for a family when their loved one is first diagnosed. Additional respite funds are available through LEARN. I know from personal experience how important respite is for the primary caregiver.

Then, we shifted gears to the March 23-25 Public Policy Forum. This year marks my ninth consecutive Forum! I'm still as excited about going as I was the first time. My sister is going with me this year and we plan to spend some quality time in our nation's capitol. The Chapter wants to send a person in the early stages and his or her caregiver to Washington, DC. I promised Ashley that I would think about possible candidates from our area.

Ashley got another phone call and had to hang up. I looked at the pile of papers on my desk: month end/year end reports with issues. Numbers buzzed through my brain relentlessly working on this brain-teasing puzzle. A one-page report that should have taken less than ten minutes to verify had turned into a full day quest for answers. Our conversation had been short—less than five minutes, but it brightened my day and reminded me that the most important things in my life were not on my desk. I had let work problems fill my mind with anxiety.

More important that comparing spreadsheets to printouts are Girl Scout cookies, basketball games, math club, and baby smiles. Important things are editing my book and submitting it to an agent. Now, an important thing is taking my Alzheimer's volunteerism to the Ambassador level.

My Oxford American Dictionary shows one definition of ambassador as "an official messenger." I have been a messenger for the Alzheimer's Association since my first contact with them before we had a diagnosis for Jim. Soon, I will be "official" but that won't make me stodgy. Being an Alzheimer's Volunteer for me is not something I do just because I want to; it's something I am compelled to do.

# Airplane Crash Survivors
## Saturday, January 17, 2009

I'm not a frequent flyer, but I fly often. When I clicked on the headlines of the US Airways crash, it was one of the strangest sights I had ever seen. The jet rested on top of the water with survivors standing on the wings waiting for their turn to be rescued. I immediately Googled the crash to see what else I could learn. The miracle story just seemed to get better and better. Then I saw a YouTube of an Airbus Crash. Wow! That was quick.

I clicked on the video and watched a plane getting lower to the ground. I was disappointed as the plane went out of sight because I wanted to see the water landing. When I thought the video would end, the jet exploded and a plume of smoke and flames shot skyward. Wrong video.

It did give me pause. Why did one jet crash and burn and the other land in water and float long enough for all passengers and crew to be rescued? What separates victims from survivors?

Why are so many people terrified of flying while others, like me, get no more excited than stepping on an elevator? It has nothing to do with bad experiences, but seems more to be something hard-wired in our brains.

I've had a few harrowing experiences aboard aircraft, but it hasn't interfered with my love of travel. When I was eighteen, I flew to Hawaii where Jim and I planned to marry while he was on R&R from Vietnam. My first flight was a non-stop out of Kansas City to San Francisco. After a breakfast of eggs benedict, the flight attendants (called stewardesses back then) picked up our trash and made sure everyone's seats were in an upright position and seatbelts securely fastened. The plane began a sharp descent and we came in for a landing.

As the plane barreled down a runway seemingly in the middle of nowhere, police cars, taxis, fire trucks and ambulances followed us. As soon as the plane stopped, an announcement came over the speakers, "Exit from the nearest exit and get into the taxis." We were herded into a building and stood beside our luggage as it was searched. Our emergency landing in Denver was a precaution because someone ("do any of you know someone who would have done such a thing?") phoned-in a bomb threat specifying our flight and destination.

In 1986, about two weeks after the Challenger explosion, I flew back to Hawaii. That time a TWA plane came so close to us that my sister swears she saw the shocked look on the pilot's face.

It is not so much experiences as our personalities that determine how we feel about life's challenges. Some of us are survivors and expect to continue moving forward with our lives. Others feel like victims and expect more catastrophes in their future.

Those of us who have loved ones with Alzheimer's, or lost loved ones to the disease, know the only survivors are the caregivers. We are the pilots who land the plane on the water and wait patiently on the wings with knowledge in our hearts that we will endure, overcome, and continue forward with our lives.

My next scheduled flight is to the Alzheimer's Association Public Policy Forum. During these hard economic times, we need to ask for continued fast-track research to find a cure for the 5.2 million Americans with Alzheimer's. It is unthinkable that all my friends with dementia are on a plane that will crash and burn. We need to adopt a survivor mentality for those with Alzheimer's, and not lose hope that science can bring them in for a safe and miraculous landing.

# Will Work for Food
## Saturday, January 24, 2009

Several years ago during another economic downturn, Jim and I had just left Wal-Mart. We didn't have a lot of money, so we had carefully selected enough groceries for the week. We stopped in a line of traffic waiting to pull onto Highway 50. A scruffy looking man carried a sign that said "Will Work for Food." Several drivers in front of us rolled down windows and handed the man money.

Jim said, "Roll down your window, Honey."

Jim was a generous sort of man, so I thought he was going to give the guy some money. We knew what hard times were firsthand. I began to rummage through my purse looking for a few dollars. Jim beckoned the man to come over, and the man leaned into my window.

Jim said, "Hey, I have a lot of work that needs to be done at my house. I can keep you busy for several days." It was true that we could use help. Jim and I were building our house with sweat equity, and we had worked on it for months, and had many more to go.

I thought maybe Jim had lost his mind. No way did I want this man at my home with my family. Besides I watch a lot of TV and was pretty sure this guy looked like serial killer material.

The man got a strange look on his face and no longer seemed the humble job seeker of a few moments before. He looked to the right. He swept his gaze to the left. "I have to go," he said. "Those people in the next car want to talk to me."

I rolled my window up and slammed down the button to lock the door in case that Charles Manson looking character changed his mind. "Are you crazy?" I asked Jim. "I wouldn't want that man to even know where we live, much less hang around for days!" I was huffy.

Jim just laughed. "Hell, there's no way that guy wants to work. He only wants a handout."

I always hated it when Jim was right. It would have suited my personality to hand the guy some money, but Jim was a man with quick judgment who could spot a scam artist a mile away.

We pulled onto the highway. "You still took a chance," I said. "I would have been scared to death if that guy had climbed in the van with us."

"Wasn't going to happen," Jim said. "You don't look for a job standing out on the street holding a sign."

I looked in the rearview mirror and saw the man back at the corner with his "Will Work for Food" sign held high as another car rolled to a stop and the window came down. Sometimes it's easier to hand over money than to judge character. In hard economic times, scam artists work hard to take your money and steal donations that could go to people who really need it.

# It's a Small World
## Sunday, February 1, 2009

"It's a small world" isn't just a slogan for Disneyland and doesn't just apply to children wearing Mickey Mouse ears. Other lands and cultures are not the mysterious settings for fairy tales and novels they once were. Now, we know people from those places, we may have toured them, or features on the Travel Channel makes us feel like we've been there.

Other than rare trips to Sedalia or Kansas City, we shopped locally when I was a child. We bought clothes at Nolting's Department Store and groceries at Cooper's. My dad was a builder and he bought building supplies at Fagen's Lumber Yard. Our choices were limited. The world was huge and Stover was just a minuscule blip on the surface.

Now, we have access to online stores and can buy merchandise in a worldwide marketplace. Our choices are unlimited. My co-worker, Brenda, found a rare 50th anniversary National Rural Electric Cooperative Association hurricane lamp on eBay. A few days later, she got a call from one of her neighbors who said, "I'll just bring it by and refund your postage." What are the odds that you buy an item off eBay and the seller is your neighbor?

The Internet makes our world smaller whether transactions are with a neighbor or someone in another country. Millions of us reconnect with old acquaintances or make new friends on the Internet every day.

How many people do you know that fell in love with a "soul mate" they met online? I watched an *NCIS* episode where Tony posed as a female to play a trick on McGee who thought he had finally met the perfect "woman." It sort of reminds you of a Brad Paisley song, doesn't it? A lot of people need Brad's disclaimer, "I'm so much cooler online."

Through Internet searches, I tracked down two of Jim's old army buddies. When Jim developed dementia, he couldn't give the information we needed to file a PTSD claim. I turned to the Internet to contact two of the men he served with in Vietnam. One man had a fairly common name, but I found a piece of paper in Jim's wallet with an address. Of course, it was unlikely he would be in the same hometown twenty-six years later. The other army buddy had an unusual name, but I had no idea where he lived. After some Internet detective work, I discovered one friend had died from alcoholism and the other lived in Maine.

When I began this blog about a year ago, I didn't expect many people would read it. Last week, my blog was viewed 222 times. Of course, that isn't much considering I potentially have a worldwide audience, but it's a lot for someone who grew up in Stover, population 757.

I often receive emails that say, "I just found your blog today." One of those emails came from my former sister-in-law. Which makes me think…it's a small, small world after all.

# Do You Think You Can, or Think You Can't?
## Friday, February 6, 2009

Jodi Stucker, Phi Beta Lambda advisor, spoke at our Business and Professional Women's Meeting last night. I was impressed by the accomplishments of State Fair Community College students. Local PBL students competed at National Competition and two placed in the top ten. One young lady won first place in computer applications!

At the end of the presentation, Jodi showed a slide of a beautiful fountain in front of their hotel in Atlanta. Across the bottom of the slide was a quote: "If you think you can, or you think you can't, you're right."— Henry Ford.

The "can do" attitude was instilled in me at an early age. My mom and dad had a hard time raising eight kids. My mom worked at a factory, and Dad farmed, drove a school bus, and worked long hours as a builder. They never threw their hands in the air and said, "Lord, how are we going to feed all these hungry mouths?" No, they just thought they could and they did.

When our kids were small, I stayed home with them while Jim earned our living. For several years when we filed our income tax, we fell below the poverty level. Strangely, we didn't really consider ourselves to be poor. We always paid our bills, and saved money when we had it to tide us through the times when we didn't. We always knew we would make it. I'm not saying we never worried, but we never let setbacks destroy our lives.

In 1976, I began classes at State Fair Community College under a program called Manpower. I had to be persistent to quality for the program because I was not the primary breadwinner in our family. The second roadblock was the counselor's insistence that with high unemployment, I should study nursing instead of secretarial. Let me tell you I was squeamish about nursing—shots, illness, all that blood... I knew nursing was not the program for me.

"You have to be top-notch to get a job in secretarial," he said. "There just aren't many jobs now. Nurses can always find work." He totally didn't understand why I wasn't jumping at the opportunity to be a nurse.

"I will be top-notch," I assured him. At State Fair, I doubled up on classes and managed to get a two-year degree in slightly more than a year. Even with high unemployment, I found a job before graduation. I was able to do it because I thought I could.

Later, the stakes became higher when Jim developed dementia. You can imagine that my squeamishness had not changed a lot over the years. Being a caregiver is much like being a nurse. You learn to deal with illness and occasionally blood. During the years of caregiving,

I basically woke up each morning chanting the mantra: "I can make it through today."

Money can't buy love or good health, but the lack of it can make life tougher. Either accept the challenge to make it through the tough times and still enjoy life, or decide you can't and sink into despair. The choice is yours—can or can't? Just remember, you will be right.

# Love is Never Out of Style
## Saturday, February 14, 2009

The movement to end Valentine's Day seems more vocal this year. Has our society become so pragmatic that we think a day devoted to love is out of style?

Roland S. Martin's commentary, "Don't be my Valentine," takes the view that since it is not a religious holiday, we shouldn't celebrate it like we do Christmas or Easter. Isn't celebrating love as religious as Santa Claus and Easter Bunnies?

Martin indicates that women have become greedy and needy for valentine's gifts while men are "pawns" who empty "their wallets in order to satisfy their lovers or those around them." Come on! Martin should get the "Grinch of Valentine's Day Award."

I cannot recall one Valentine's Day in my life when I wanted more than a card. Expecting or even wanting a dozen roses was never on my heart-shaped radar. Jim often purchased a single red rose at the local convenience store and personally delivered it to me at work. Sweet! I could have cared less if a co-worker received a room full of roses. All that mattered to me was the man I loved still wanted me to be his valentine. I'm afraid that I, and millions of other women, do not fit Martin's stereotype.

Some historians link the origin of Valentine's Day to an ancient Roman pagan holiday to honor Juno, the Goddess of women and marriage. The Christian version is based on a different scenario. Emperor Claudius II devised a plan to build his army by prohibiting marriage. The idea was that soldiers were not volunteering to fight and die for the emperor because they were reluctant to leave their sweethearts behind. The legend is that Valentine was executed on February 14, 269 A.D. for performing marriage in opposition to Emperor Claudius orders. In 496, Pope Gelasius set aside the day of the priest's death to honor St. Valentine for being a martyr for love.

Historians claim the dates of many Christian holidays, including Christmas, were chosen to coincide with Roman holidays. Of course, it's possible that the Romans had so many holidays it was hard to miss one of them. Is February 14, pagan or Christian? My question to Martin is—what does the Bible call the greatest of all?

Whatever the origins of the holiday, love is never out of style. It is a celebration of the heart and doesn't inconvenience anyone. We don't close the banks and post offices for it. Happy Valentine's Day and may your world be filled with love.

# Health Fairs Make Me Sick!
## Saturday, February 21, 2009

This week we had our annual health fair at work to collect the necessary data for a discount on our insurance premium. Don't get me wrong, I'm a firm believer in discounts and feel fortunate to have good health insurance. When Jim developed dementia, our health insurance allowed us to choose the best treatment options available.

My first objection is calling this experience a "fair." I remember the Stover Fair with its thrilling rides: Ferris Wheel, the Bullet, Teacups, Swings, carnies, hamburgers cooked by the American Legion, and marching with my classmates in the parade. At this health "fair" I didn't see a single carnival ride.

Instead, I arrive at work well before 7:00 a.m., grumpy, because I haven't had my morning coffee. The highlight of the health fair is to give up a vial of blood to get current numbers for the online health survey. Really, it isn't the un-fun fair that gets us the discount—it's filling out that darn survey.

All of us employees have been successfully bribed with Donna's biscuits and Kathy's sausage gravy. Man-oh-man, the building smells good. Is that the scent of coffee wafting through the air?

Soon, nurses line up, and with assembly line precision, shuffle employees to be weighed, get blood drawn, grab a blood pressure, and glaucoma screen. I give Nurse Lana a hug—she and I went to school together in Stover. We both know this isn't a real fair, at least, not like the ones in our memories.

A long line snakes in front of the nurses, but there is no waiting at the glaucoma screening station. I look at the green light and blink as air puffs into my eyes. My reading is above the normal range. Not a good way to start the day.

I decide to work awhile and come back when the line is shorter. I take a cup of water to my desk and hunt for a printout that has mysteriously disappeared. I sip my water and try to ignore the headache behind my eyes.

Finally, I risk the line again and it is much shorter. By now, my head has progressed to a dull ache.

Lana motions me to weigh-in. It's pretty humiliating to step on the scales in front of your co-workers. I didn't need the scales and a handy-dandy chart to tell me my BMI is too high.

Next stop, blood draw. Wheee, now we're talking thrill. The nurse drawing blood is falling behind so Lana offers to draw mine. Although I've been guzzling water for three hours, she can't find a vein. They are all in hiding. She looks at the other arm. No vein, no luck.

30

Lana says, "I really don't want to take it out of the back of your hand."

"I really don't want you to either," I said. Been there, done that. It hurts a lot more than the arm.

Back to the left arm. Finally, she sees a faint glimpse of blue and sticks in her tiniest needle. No luck. After consulting with the other nurse, they decide I need to drink more water.

I go fill my cup and drink two cups of water. I go ahead and have my blood pressure checked. It is high, of course.

I drop back by the blood nurse. She looks at my arms and shakes her head. Then, she inspects the backs of my hands and now those veins are hiding too. She tells me to drink water and let her look again in ten minutes. My head pounds and I start to feel as nauseous as I did the last time I rode the Teacups. Finally, I say, "Let's go for it." I'm hungry and caffeine deprived.

She slaps the blue band around one arm and then the other. I make serious fists, trying to get the veins to pop up. She sticks the needle in. Nothing happens. Lana watches as the nurse tries another spot and when she gets close to the vein, it rolls. She prods around with the needle. "You may need to come into the office," she says.

"There it is!" Lana says. Thank goodness, blood is filling the vial.

Finally! I take my golden ticket and head for the biscuits and gravy. You'd think that with my cholesterol, blood sugar, weight issues, I would eat fruit instead. No way. I filled my plate and headed back to the kitchen to get a cup of coffee.

By now, my head feels like a ticking time bomb. I take everything to my desk because I still have to find that darn printout and get a day-and-a-half worth of work done today. After I eat and drink coffee, my head still hurts. I'm not the only one with a sick headache. Brenda, Kathy, and Donna all say their heads hurt too.

After two ibuprofen tablets, lunch and a diet Pepsi, my headache finally abates. Now that I feel better, I begin to find humor in the whole situation. The health fair made us sick!

The bright point in the whole heath fair/discount experience is we don't have to fast for the survey.

# Snow Isn't as Much Fun as It Used to Be
## Saturday, February 28, 2009

When I was growing up, a big snow was a lot of fun. On snow days, we would drag out the wooden sleds with the metal runners.

The Ozark hills provided perfect sledding terrain. The road formed a long sloping hill on the north side of our house and a short, steep hill on the south side. The problem with the north hill was the long walk to the top before the downhill ride. The other hill was a shorter walk and a faster ride.

It wasn't long before we figured out we could fairly fly downhill if we kick started the sled and plopped belly down and head first. Well, there was the time my brother, Donnie, ran his sled off the road crashing headlong into the barn. His broken nose ended his sledding that day, but it didn't slow down the rest of us.

All this reminiscing began this morning when the forecast called for five inches of snow, and I needed to be in Fulton, MO, for our Lifelines for Women program. Earlier in the week we had seventy-degree weather, and I breathed a sigh of relief that Cate and I weren't out of our minds when we selected the last day of February for the retreat.

Yesterday, I heard the forecast—snow, snow, and more snow for Sedalia. I woke up this morning relieved to see the predicted snow had not fallen. I showered and relaxed for a few minutes until I noticed the ground was white. By the time I left home, snow salted the earth and began to accumulate to fulfill the meteorologist's prediction.

I expected the side roads to be slick, but was confident 65 Highway would be clear. Wrong. It was snow packed and traffic was running a smooth 30 miles per hour. OK. Surely, the Interstate would be plowed. Wrong again. The ditches were littered with cars, trucks, and trailers. I got caught behind a vehicle traveling so slow that a snow plow passed us. Have you ever been on the wrong side of a snow plow? I might as well have been in a blizzard. My wipers iced up and left blurry streaks all over my windshield. Eventually, I drove out of the storm and onto beautiful, dry pavement.

The drive home was normal until I turned off the highway. The gravel road was challenging with its two beaten paths and pile of snow in the middle. The closer I got to home, the deeper the snow.

Finally, I pulled into my detached garage, put on my snow boots and tromped through six inches of snow to my door. Is it my imagination or is walking in deep snow a lot like walking in quicksand?

Snow just isn't as much fun as it used to be. Or, are my memories a little deceptive? If I thought hard enough, would I recall numb fingers and toes from the bone-chilling cold? I have forgotten any spills, bumps and bruises, but recall the fun of outdoor wintertime activities. In my memories, I don't think about lugging the sled to the top of the hill, I only remember the thrill of the downhill ride.

# Reality TV: The Final Rose—or Not
## Saturday, March 7, 2009

Just when you think reality TV can't get more unreal, *The Bachelor* might as well have passed out dead roses instead of red roses. Don't get me wrong, I believe in love. I just don't believe love happens because a producer chooses a group of attractive women to act like idiots over one eligible male. The Bachelor in question doesn't seem to have many requirements, including a stable personality.

I'm not much of a reality TV fan. I used to watch people eat spiders and leap off tall buildings on *Fear Factor* while I fed Jim at the nursing home. Not for a million dollars would I jump between skyscrapers or dive into a tank of snakes.

*Survivor* has never interested me. I watched the *Great Race* a few seasons and found it to be entertaining at times. *American Idol* is my favorite! At least that requires a degree of talent. Thank goodness Tatiana was sent home because she gets on my nerves.

I've become bored with the multitude of bachelors over the years and admit that several seasons have slipped by when I haven't watched a single episode. I could just barf if I watch one more hot tub scene or a woman wailing and gnashing her teeth because, "I'll always love him, but he didn't give me a rose!" Get real. How do you fall in love with a shallow, one-dimensional player who is coming on to twenty-four other women at the same time?

The camera caught all the details of the dramatic, long-goodbye when Molly got the boot. Her tragic and crushed figure rode into the sunset in a limousine. Tears glistened on her cheeks and her eyes brimmed. "He's making a big mistake," she sobs.

Jason shows his own anguish by bawling his eyes out before he regains his composure in time to fall on one knee and propose to Melissa. They jump into the water wearing their good clothes. I suppose ruined outfits are a small price to pay for the artistic value of the happy couple, and little boy, Ty, frolicking in the water.

Jason proves to be fickle-hearted and dumps his fiancé on national TV to re-choose his second choice, Molly. He said he just couldn't quit thinking about Molly. Thinking is not Jason's strong suit.

Melissa, needless to say, is a little ticked at him. She speaks of herself in the third person, which makes you wonder about her stability. The drama continues when Molly makes her entrance and learns of the new developments in the love triangle. Molly could have been a credit to all womankind had she looked him in the eye and said, "I am *so* over you!" Instead her caught-in-the-headlights eyes dart as if she expects someone to yell, "Just kidding!" The show ends with

Molly and Jason falling into each other's arms and
locking lips.

Do any of these people know what love is? Maybe, but
more likely, not. No pressure, but fall in love and
propose by the final episode. I think it's more likely the
bachelor just tosses a coin. It's a game, and the choice
doesn't really matter. He doesn't plan to really marry
the girl anyway, and by the time the final episode airs,
the happy couple is not a couple anymore.

Yes, I believe in love and I believe in reality, but I'm
skeptical that love and reality TV are a marriage made
in heaven.

# Missouri Advocates at State Capitol for Memory Day
## Saturday, March 14, 2009

I am an Alzheimer's Advocate and participate in Memory Day at the state capitol in Jefferson City. Wednesday, I made my annual trip to speak to my legislators. My sister-in-law, Ginger, went with me this year.

The biggest challenge of Memory Day is finding a place to park. How every parking space within miles of the state capitol can be full is a mystery to me. I looked for a parking place close to the Truman Building.

My first mistake was trying to go in the entrance that is now barricaded with pylons to discourage terrorists, I suppose. I went around the block only to discover the other side had only an exit. I shot across a bridge to nowhere, turned around in a parking lot, and drove back around the block.

I trolled the parking lot while Ginger kept a sharp eye out for an empty slot. After cruising all around, we exited that parking lot and entered the one across the street for a more realistic chance. Finally, in the second to last row, we found an empty parking space. With perfect positioning, we were able to exit the car without stepping into the lake-size mud puddle that surrounded the front half of the car.

My cell phone rang just as I hopped over the puddle. It was Ike Skelton's office setting up a time for our visit during the Public Policy Forum in Washington, DC. I juggled my bag and wrote the time in my calendar.

A March wind gusted around us as we headed toward the capitol building. Ginger and I wore pictures of Jim over our hearts. In the photo, Jim wears his Stetson and looks like a movie star or country-western recording artist.

After a short training session, we found a seat in the rotunda for the ceremony. The ceremony opened with a "Hello" song and drummers. After the awards and recognition, we began our legislative visits. We made a statement by donning purple "Alzheimer's Association" sashes. It's really hard to ignore 240 people wearing "beauty queen" sashes!

During our visits, the senate debated and passed SB176 which calls for the creation of a Missouri Alzheimer's State Plan Task Force. This Task Force will assess the current and future impact of Alzheimer's disease and examine the resources available for families affected by dementia. After their assessment, the Task Force will develop and implement recommendations to help Missourians take a proactive approach to make life better for the 110,000 Missourians with dementia, their caregivers, and families.

Our other objective is to maintain funding for Alzheimer's Service Grants. The grants help the four Missouri Chapters continue their important mission to provide services and support to families who are on the Alzheimer's journey.

I consider myself to be a poster child for these services. Respite funds provided by the Mid-Missouri Chapter were my only financial support while Jim lived at home. The Alzheimer's support group and educational programs helped me be a better caregiver. As a person who's been there and done that, I know the life-changing possibilities of the $539,000 service grants. These grants save Medicaid dollars by delaying admittance to expensive nursing homes. As advocates we asked our senators and representatives to support these two priorities.

We make a difference when we share our personal stories with our legislators. The heart of Memory Day isn't about politics, it's about the people we know and love who are living with dementia, and our living memories of the ones lost to the disease.

# What Would Jim Do?
## Thursday, March 19, 2009

Jim was a disabled veteran and received compensation from the government. While he was in long-term care, I sent his Veterans and Social Security checks to the nursing home. Jim died in 2005 and the checks stopped.

I was surprised to receive a letter from the Veterans Administration admitting that some surviving spouses had not received the veteran's compensation for the month the veteran died. Apparently, after all this time, the VA realized they should have sent me one more check.

Since almost four years had passed before I received the letter, I wasn't expecting the check anytime soon. To my surprise, it came a few weeks later.

In my mind this was Jim's money and my first question was, *what would Jim do?* We were married more than 35 years, and I had a good idea what his wishes would be.

Jim had received a few windfalls over the years, and he always knew exactly what he wanted to do. Whether it was a $700 winning lottery ticket or a $10,000 settlement, he never considered spending the money on himself. He always had someone in the back of his mind that needed cash more than he did.

It took me a while to understand his philosophy. We went through a lot of hard times when we were younger, and often I felt like we needed the money. He always had faith we would get by, but he wasn't so sure about everyone else.

Somewhere along life's journey, I learned that the more you give, the more you receive. I'm not talking about gift exchange. Jim didn't care for or even believe in gift exchanges. When he gave, it was never, ever because he expected something in return. It was because he just felt it in his heart. He would open his billfold and hand over his last dollar to someone he loved.

He wouldn't have wanted this unexpected check to be put in the bank. I know he would want the grandkids to have something from "Grandpa Jim" so that was the easy part. The more I thought about it, I knew where he would want the rest of it to go.

It makes me feel good to know Jim's giving spirit can reach out and lend a helping hand to people he loved. In my memory, I can see him smile and his eyes light up. I can't think of a better use for Jim's check than to honor his legacy of love.

# Purple Passion for Alzheimer's at the Public Policy Forum
## Saturday, March 28, 2009

When Jim and I became engaged April 5, 1969, our colors were purple and yellow. Jim would tell me, "I love you with a purple passion," and then he would add, "with a yellow racing stripe." You have to realize that in 1969 racing stripes were really cool.

Purple is the signature color of the Alzheimer's Association. I really don't know why they chose purple, but the color can still be associated with passion.

My sister, Roberta, and I arrived in Washington, DC, a few days before the Alzheimer's Association Public Policy Forum. We visited historic landmarks and attended services in the National Cathedral on Sunday morning. Cherry blossoms verged on blooming, and we couldn't have asked for better weather.

Through past experience, I've found the most essential item for DC is comfortable shoes. Even with comfortable shoes, we managed to return each night with weary legs and aching feet. Everything in Washington, DC, is bigger than life—including the distance between buildings and monuments.

We joined more than five hundred advocates to bring passion to Capitol Hill. Twenty-four delegates from Missouri experienced the Alzheimer's Association's

21st Annual Forum. Four advocates in our group have been diagnosed with early or younger-onset Alzheimer's.

Mike Splaine, Alzheimer's Association Advocacy guru, said because the Alzheimer's crisis is gradual it is in danger of being overlooked. He said we needed passion and intensity to bring about change and take steps to make Alzheimer's disease a national priority.

Maria Shriver, first lady of California, wasn't satisfied to merely attend the forum—she wanted to experience the forum. She made her first appearance at the candlelight vigil Monday evening. After speakers passionately talked about their journeys, we lit our candles of remembrance and hope for a future without Alzheimer's.

On Tuesday, Maria introduced a preview of an upcoming four-part HBO special about Alzheimer's. The heartbreaking message ended with the word HOPELESS truncated to read HOPE.

Our group of 500 stormed Capitol Hill with purple sashes making us stand out from the crowd. We visited our respective senators and representatives to speak with one voice.

Our legislative "ask" was streamlined this year to three issues. Research was at the top of the list. We asked for an additional $250 million this year and another $250 million in 2010 to reach our illusive $1 billion goal. The annual total cost of Alzheimer's is $148 billion. If $1 billion in research funding could reduce the annual cost by a small percentage it would be a wise investment.

Secondly, we asked for an Alzheimer's Solutions Project Office. This office would be charged with leading a national effort to reengineer dementia care delivery.

We also asked for a phase out of the Social Security two-year waiting period for Medicare. Expensive diagnostic tests are sometimes delayed due to the waiting period. Early drug intervention may also be postponed past the time when it does the most good.

The *2009 Alzheimer's Disease Facts and Figures* highlights the prevalence of the disease. Alzheimer's is a family disease, and every 70 seconds another family begins this journey. Seventy percent of the 5.3 million Americans with Alzheimer's are cared for by 9.9 million unpaid caregivers.

Alzheimer's statistics can be alarming, but personal stories are the heartbeat behind the numbers. When a legislator looks into a caregiver's sad eyes or into the confused gaze of a person with dementia, we become more than a number. We humanize the emotional and physical drain of a degenerative and fatal brain disease.

Jim was in a nursing home when I made my first trip to Washington DC. His dementia often made me feel helpless and hopeless. The trips helped rejuvenate my spirit and gave me purpose.

I am friends with many amazing people that advocacy brought into my life. Being an advocate is personally rewarding, and I believe it is important for those with Alzheimer's and their families.

This was my ninth trip to Washington, DC, as an advocate. Jim died in 2005, but I continue to make the trip in his memory. Each year, when I prepare for the Public Policy Forum, I take my purple passion and pack comfortable shoes.

# Clown Noses, Laughter and Tears
## Saturday, April 4, 2009

I heard rumors that the speaker at our Business and Professional Women's meeting, Vickie Weaver, had asked for clown noses for each person in attendance. My first reaction was a mental rolling of eyes and words raced through my brain that I won't put in writing.

I've always enjoyed humor and having fun, but usually avoid acting silly. Clown noses sounded pretty ridiculous.

Vickie presented the first part of her program on "The Art of Laughter" touting the therapeutic benefits of laughter. We've all heard about life threatening diseases being cured after a person watched several days of slapstick comedy.

The dreaded moment arrived and clown noses were distributed. We opened plastic wrappers and plunked the red sponge noses over our real noses. Immediately, cell phones were removed from purses to take advantage of this photo op. I seriously hope there are not pictures of me on YouTube wearing a red Sponge-Bob nose.

I'm pretty sure our honored guests for the evening—a table of men, the chicken fryers from last fall's fundraiser—thought we had lost our minds. A couple of them tentatively put on their noses, but they didn't jump up like the rest of us to learn a variety of laughs.

My favorite was the one that ended with throwing our hands in the air and shouting "Wheeeeeeeeeeeee!" Other favorites were the "handshake" and the "thumbs up" laugh.

I laughed so hard my sides hurt and the muscles on the back part of my head began to ache. I'm sure the good endorphins helped us through the serious topic that dominated our business meeting. We discussed the imminent demise of the ninety-year-old BPW organization we all know and love. Our group is determination to continue with our local's good work even if it requires a name change. Our BPW local supports community programs year round and annually awards scholarships.

Vickie's timing was perfect to remind us of the importance of not just a smile or chuckle, but a real full-body laugh. It is impossible to take yourself too seriously while you wear a clown nose. Clown noses and laughter put troubles into perspective.

After a blustery, cold Thursday, Friday morning was bright with the slight chill of a Colorado summer day, the kind of morning that always makes me miss Jim. It was my day off and I had time to think about personal pressing issues. My broken dryer topped the list. My sister-in-law, Ginger, had already dried two loads of clothes for me. Now, I needed to figure out how to get the dryer repaired or replaced.

As I poured my first cup of coffee, a moment of utter sadness over life's losses brought tears to my eyes. I thought about how much Jim loved a cup of coffee. He drank his coffee black. He wanted it steaming hot, so he used a thick cup and drank a half-cup at a time. After his cup of coffee he would have fixed the dryer, and it wouldn't have been my problem.

I'm not usually one to weep over what "should-a-could-a" been, so I brushed aside the tears to answer the phone. A friend told me he was on the way over to look at my dryer. My spirits lifted, and while I drank my first cup of coffee, I enjoyed the lovely spring day. I began to hum—life can be fun regardless of those pesky day-to-day problems.

I pulled my clown nose out of my purse. Should I just pop the nose on and practice my "Wheeeee!" laugh? Nah! No sense in being silly.

# Teddy Bear Smiles and Not So Sweet Dreams
## Saturday, April 11, 2009

Like many other children, my granddaughter has a favorite stuffed animal she wants to hug while she sleeps. Her bedtime companion is Finney, a Build-a-Bear puppy born in Branson. From the time she warmed his "heart" in her hands, Finney has been her nighttime companion.

Last weekend at bedtime, her question was, "Where's Finney?"

Her mom, Stacey, told her, "He's in the car with Daddy."

"But Daddy is at the races!" my granddaughter said. "Finney is alone in the car. I feel so bad!" She buried her face in my lap.

We spent several minutes reassuring her that Finney would be OK. My granddaughter insisted, "He's afraid of the dark!"

Stacey handed her a big Teddy bear. "You can sleep with this bear until Daddy gets home."

"Why don't you hug him?" I asked her. "He hardly ever gets hugs." The snuggly brown bear had a big sewn-on smile and an orange ribbon around his neck.

My granddaughter hugged him tight. When she held him out to look at him, she said, "Oh, Grandma Linda, his smile is bigger now. Look! He's so happy!"

I finished a few things before going into my bedroom. She was fast asleep on my bed with the bear hugged to her heart.

With such a pleasant evening, I expected a good night's sleep. Instead, that was the first night of a week-long series of bad dreams. Night after night, I dreamed about packing for a trip. Nothing seemed to go right in the dreams: the van showed up to take me to the airport before I had my suitcases packed, I couldn't find my passport, my purse was missing. The scenarios changed but the disturbing dreams continued all week.

Last night, I slept restfully without any bad dreams. I awakened to discover my arms wrapped around the Teddy bear—his nose to my nose. Daylight flowed through the windows, and I could easily see his smiling face.

Not quite ready to wake up, I closed my eyes for a few seconds and thought about the weekend ahead. Easter weekend will be a celebration of Easter egg hunts and services at the Mathewson Center. But the best part of the weekend is my sons and their families plan to join me for Easter services. With our hectic lives, it seems we are seldom together.

With my eyes still closed, I thought about other Easters—the time Jim and his brother-in-law, Dennis, caught a stringer of fish; hiding Easter eggs too well and helping the kids find them; huge family meals at my mother-in-law's house; dressing the kids up in their Easter outfits, and a rush of other memories about Easters past.

I opened my eyes and smiled at the Teddy bear I still held in my arms. He smiled back, of course, with his sewn-on happy face. Maybe my granddaughter was right—his smile seemed a bit bigger than it had been. Well, at the thought of the weekend ahead, I know mine certainly was.

# Memories of a Rocky Mountain Morning
## Sunday, April 19, 2009

My alarm awakened me Saturday morning at the unreasonable hour of 6 a.m. I attempted to clear the fog from my brain to figure out why the darn thing was disturbing my sleep. I shut off the alarm and settled back on my Memory Foam pillow to listen to the radio while I contemplated the rude awakening.

After a few minutes, I remembered I needed to be at work by 7:30. While I tried to convince myself to jump out of bed, the DJ played Vince Gill's song, "Rest High on That Mountain."

What a fitting song for the fourth anniversary of Jim's death. The epithet on Jim's niche at the Veteran's Cemetery is "Rest High on That Mountain."

The anniversary had been bearing on my mind for the entire week. I thought about it on Monday the 13th, which seemed much like a Friday the 13th. I was at home that day, but instead of relaxing, I spent the day working on various projects. Tuesday was a hectic workday with deadlines to complete before noon on Wednesday. I ran into problems, but managed to finish my reports before Brenda and I left for the accountant's meeting in Kansas City. By the time I got back into the office Friday, I was mentally and physically exhausted.

On this gloomy Saturday morning, all I wanted to do was sleep, but the Vince Gill song brought back a flood of emotions. In my memories, I see Jim sitting on the rock ledge overlooking the Big Horn Meadow in the Rocky Mountain National Forest. Jim plays his guitar and sings a song about Colorado while I videotape him. Tourists and chipmunks watch in hushed silence. One brave chipmunk runs up Jim's arm and perches on his shoulder.

The Rocky Mountains soothed Jim's soul. He liked nothing better than making coffee on a camp stove in Moraine Park. He would have kicked back in a lawn chair, sipped coffee by the campfire, and waited for the sun to peek through the mountains.

Jim didn't need an alarm clock to wake him in the mornings. He was never a sleepyhead like me.

I remember Jim telling me "Rest High on That Mountain" was written as a tribute to Vince Gill's brother who died too young after a lingering illness. The song spoke to Jim's heart.

Our minds play tricks on us, but I can't help but think that Jim told me the history of the song on one of the many Saturday mornings we sat propped up on our pillows while we drank our first cup of coffee.

One of the things I loved most about our life together were quiet mornings when we had our "together" time to engage in contemplative conversations. At that time, Jim never suspected he would someday have a disease that would steal these moments from his memory.

As I lay in bed, I didn't think about that day four years ago, but instead remembered our ordinary lives fifteen years ago. When the song finished, I walked into the kitchen to start a pot of coffee. I opened the blinds to see a gentle rain falling. The redbuds are bloomed and tiny flowers peek through the grass. It looks like a Colorado morning.

"Rest High on That Mountain" seems to be a message from Jim. He always said that death was closing one door and opening another. I believe he wants me to know that although his death is heartbreaking for his family it is not the end; it is a continuance of life for all of us.

# Stand Up and Be Counted
## Monday, April 27, 2009

Last weekend I attended my second annual BPW State Conference. It was a busy and productive time. I thought I might be expelled from BPW for standing up for my strong—perhaps pigheaded—beliefs.

I learned from the best the importance of being true to myself. Sometimes Jim exasperated me with his determination to stand up for his "principals." I tried to get him to lighten up and admit that in a democracy, the majority ruled. No way! When he knew something was right, he defended his position. When I tried to reason with him, he merely declared, "That's against my principals."

My problem with BPW had nothing to do with our state or local organizations. I am proud of my local Business and Professional Women's Club. They are great women to work with and, boy, are we ever a busy group! We have activities, hold fundraisers, and award scholarships. The ladies in our local are my friends and I care about them.

Even Jim with his principals, would have said, "If it ain't broke, don't fix it." Unfortunately, BPW/USA is broken. My Jim-like round of stubbornness began when BPW/USA came up with a plan to charge a license fee for the BPW name.

Our national organization has made some bad business decisions and is on the brink of bankruptcy. They lost nearly $200,000 on the national conference last year and then lost touch with the very women they were created to serve. After months of pleas for more money from our incredibly shrinking organization, BPW/USA finally realized the members couldn't bail them out of their mess.

I'll spare you the details, but now BPW members are voting on a merger between BPW/USA and BPW Foundation. This is the same foundation that recently gave BPW/USA $500,000, but suspended scholarships for 2009-2010. Needless to say, that didn't set well with a lot of members.

The merger plan got worse. BPW/USA trademarked all their programs and the use of the BPW logo and even the letters *BPW*. This trademark was approved in January 2009. Why would they do such a thing? To protect the trademark, they said. In reality, it was to charge an annual license fee of $40 per person to any woman who wanted to remain a "BPW" member and continue the proud tradition of our foremothers.

What if we didn't want to pay the hostage fee to use our own name? BPW/USA's response was to advise us to check with our Secretary of State to take the necessary steps to change state and local names. The Missouri Federation of Business and Professional Women's Clubs, Inc. was chartered in 1938. Our legal council advised us that this is our name and we don't have to change it.

BPW was born ninety years ago in St. Louis by a group of women who stood up for their rights and to promote equality and fairness for women in the workplace. These forward-looking women were not afraid to stand up for their sisters and themselves.

Our Missouri women have led the charge for the past ninety years. This weekend, we stood up for the organization we love and for the opportunity to revitalize and reorganize our group.

After we discussed the proposed resolution to disassociate our Missouri Federation from BPW/USA, we were asked to stand if we supported the resolution. The room was filled with my BPW sisters who stood up for what was right.

I believe BPW/USA underestimated the caliber of women who make up their membership. It wasn't just the newer members who stood up, but long-term members who have been involved in the organization for decades. Women with integrity, courage, and principals stood up to be counted.

# The Over-Fifty Diagnostic Test
## Saturday, May 2, 2009

My family doctor, bless his heart, is looking out for my
overall health and decided I should have a colonoscopy.
Geeze, it certainly sounded like a lot of fun, but
somehow I had dodged the experience for more than
fifty years.

I had just reminded him I needed my annual
mammogram and although that is pretty much having
your breasts pancaked, it is not unbearable. To be
perfectly honest, I had never heard anyone say anything
good about a colonoscopy.

I knew I was in trouble when the Miralax concoction
filled my pitcher. Holy smokes, how was I supposed to
drink that much liquid in two and a half hours? When I
make something I really like, sun tea, for example, I
usually throw out about half of it after three days.

The five o'clock hour arrived and I faced off with the
first eight ounces. I drank it in about five minutes. I
charted a schedule on my junior legal pad at fifteen
minute intervals and planned to be done before
*American Idol*. I began to think that contrary to popular
opinion, the prep really wasn't worse than the test.

I congratulated myself on not having to drink the gallon
of gunk they tried to give Jim when he was in the
hospital between nursing homes. He had been kicked

out of one home and after nearly a month in "regenerations" we had found another home for him. The hospital decided to investigate his rectal bleeding before discharging him. They assigned Eric and me the task of getting the gallon of liquid down him. After a few swallows, Jim gagged, clamped his mouth shut, and refused to drink it.

"It isn't going to happen," Eric said. He tracked down the doctor and told him Jim would not drink the nasty stuff.

"We'll have to force it down him then," the doctor said. "He needs this test."

No way were we going to allow that! Jim's life was difficult enough without someone dumping liquids down him. I knew he would vomit and possibly choke on it. Against the hospitals' recommendations, we signed a waiver to skip the test.

I thought about Jim and drank my second glass as easily as the first. By the time I finished the third glass, my stomach sloshed and felt bloated. I began to feel queasy. I decided to call my daughter-in-law, Shawna, who is a student nurse. Eric answered the phone.

"Ask Shawna what happens if I throw up," I said.

After consulting with her, he told me, "That's not good. Try to keep it down."

My stomach had other plans. I called back later. "Part of it came back up."

"Do you want us to bring you more Miralax?" he asked.

"No!" I began to look at each glass with dread.

"Then quit being a kid. Suck it up and deal with it. Shawna says it would be better to drink it a little slower and get it all down." Even through my queasiness, I had to smile at Eric's "suck it up" lecture. How many times have I heard that from him?

I threw up again, but managed to drink the rest of it. Now, I worried all night that I hadn't gotten enough of the solution down. According to Dr. Google, I would have to begin all over again if I didn't follow directions exactly.

I made it to bed around midnight and was up at 4 a.m. to get into the hospital on time. Ginger drove and reported in as my designated driver.

The nurses were very nice and covered me with warm blankets. They inserted an IV lock and soon after, I exchanged good mornings with the doctor.

"How are you today?" he asked.

"Well, I'd rather be fishing, and I don't even fish," I replied.

Soon they started the drug, and I began to feel lightheaded. I shut my eyes for a few seconds and then opened them again. I could see a monitor. I watched as the doctor used a shiny loop to snare a small polyp. I was so fascinated with what they were doing, the time passed quickly.

The nurse gave me a cup of coffee and some ice water to see if I could keep it down. Anesthetic of any kind usually makes me violently ill. The coffee made me queasy, but I decided it was because hospital coffee is usually on the nasty side. I had been alert throughout the procedure and thought they must not have given me much.

I was starving after a day on liquids. "Let's go get breakfast," I said to Ginger.

At the restaurant, I ordered biscuits and gravy. Before the food came, I rushed to the restroom to upchuck. Luckily I was alone so I didn't create a swine flu panic.

I boxed up my breakfast and Ginger drove me home. I spent the day sleeping and vomiting. I went to bed at nine o'clock and felt normal the next morning.

The prep really was worse than the test. In fact, the test was a piece of cake compared to the aftereffects of the anesthetic.

# When Pigs Fly: Swine Flu Immunization
## Friday, May 8, 2009

One of the advantages of getting older is I don't panic as easily as I did when I was younger. I think it's a combination of slower reaction time and the reality that I just don't have as much to lose anymore.

All this media frenzy over the swine flu reminds me of what I consider its culpability in my own brush with death. The ambiguous "its" can refer to swine flu and/or the media.

I was a lot younger in 1976 and so were my children. Eric was six and Rob was only four. Swine flu had reared its ugly head, and to protect us from harm, a massive immunization program was implemented. We were warned that since we had no immunity to this deadly virus, all able bodied Americans should be immunized. It sounded almost like our patriotic duty to do so. At the least, it seemed like our parental duty to protect our children.

Jim and I had a disagreement over the immunization.

"I'll take my chances with the flu," Jim said. "It sounds like scare tactics to me. Somebody is going to make a whole lot of money out of this."

"Well, I'm getting the shot. I'd feel just awful if I caught the flu and gave it to the kids," I argued. I played the guilt card, and asked, "You won't even do this for the safety of our kids?"

"It's just a bunch of hogwash," he said.

My motherly instincts overrode Jim's common sense, not to mention my own. I should have known that if you drove up in a car, stuck your arm out the window and had someone shoot an untested vaccine in your arm, it couldn't be good. But I did it. I can't remember just where the location of the drive-thru shot took place, but I think it might have been a bank.

I was all right for a few days after the immunization for swine flu, and I figured life would return to normal. I slept better for a few nights smug in the knowledge that I had done all I could to protect Rob and Eric.

About a week later, I began to develop some rather strange symptoms. I was fatigued and overcome with a general malaise. I barely made it through the day. My arms and legs seemed heavy, my head pounded behind my eyes, and my body ached. I wanted to sleep all the time. I was sure I would shake the mysterious ailment in a few days.

Days passed. Each day I struggled just to function. Then, a few weeks passed. We didn't have health insurance, and I figured my vague complaints wouldn't help my doctor figure out what was wrong with me. I remember being so despondent that I held a bottle of

pills in my hand and considered taking them all.
Instead, I just took a double dose and slept some more.

After six weeks, I began to feel slightly stronger each
day and within a couple of months, the mysterious
illness vanished without a trace.

I never connected my health issues to the swine flu
vaccination, until the dangers of mass immunization
began to make headlines. More people died from the
immunization than from the swine flu.

I recently read an article in the paper that the swine flu,
or the politically correct H1N1 virus, may not be as bad
as originally feared. The comforting word was that next
fall an immunization may be available for it.

Well, I'll be immunized for swine flu when pigs fly! I'd
rather take my chances with the flu. Something tells me
I might have a whole lot of immunity.

# Lessons Learned from Scott the Piano Guy
## Saturday, May 16, 2009

I was flipping through the channels recently and saw a PBS broadcast featuring Scott the Piano Guy. I don't own or play a piano, but something told me this wasn't an ordinary show, so I decided to watch it.

Scott begins his lessons by asking his studio audience, "Do any of you want to be a classic pianist?" No one raised a hand. When he asked, "Would any of you like to come home from work and play a favorite tune on the piano?" all hands reached high.

The Piano Guy has a unique method of teaching the piano, and believes anyone can learn to play in days or weeks, rather than years of lessons. He is the first to admit he is not the best piano player. He begins by demonstrating that it makes no difference which fingers you use to play the chords. The funny thing about the piano, it sounds the same regardless of which fingers you use.

Scott demonstrates how to find the mysterious (to those of us who do not play) middle C. He holds his hands out to touch both ends of the piano and falls forward onto the keys. "When I center myself at the piano," he says, "my nose hits middle C." Mystery solved.

Scott is entertaining, but he gave me much more to think about than playing the piano. First, when you tackle a problem, you need to decide on your goal. Do you want to spend years playing scales on the keyboard, or just play the darn thing? Do you want to be perfect, or will you cut yourself some slack?

Second, when you have a job to do, you can meticulously follow all the rules. Or, you can be like Scott the Piano Guy and do it your way and write new rules.

I think every caregiver can gain wisdom from Scott the Piano Guy. What is your caregiving goal? I will venture a guess that it is to take the best care you can of your loved one. You don't care about being the world's best caregiver, or plan on being a professional. Let's face it, when you become a caregiver, you can't spend years practicing before you know what you are doing. You learn to be quick, think on your feet and be creative.

As a caregiver, you can't possibly know all the rules, much less follow them. You will find yourself making them up as you progress from day-to-day. Besides when your loved one has dementia, you learn that what worked yesterday may work today but not tomorrow.

Scott the Piano Guy is successful because he is innovative. I can't think of a better attribute for successful caregivers. When people with dementia can no longer come to your world, you need to go to theirs.

If you learn to reassure your loved one and have a positive outlook, it helps both of you through a tough situation. You can be the best caregiver for your loved one without being the world's best caregiver.

Be kind to yourself and have a little fun. Rather than argue over what the rules say must be done at a particular time, go for a walk and pick a few flowers. Remember, it's not the finesse and technique that matters, it's the results. If you make the best of each day and seek out moments of joy, everyone is happier.

# Honor our Everyday Heroes
## Saturday, May 23, 2009

Memorial Day is a time to pause and think about heroes and to honor those who have died in our nation's wars. At least, that was the original purpose.

It stands to reason that we would use the day to also honor other loved ones. My Grandma Whittle called the holiday "Decoration Day." She and Grandpa loaded up a picnic lunch and went to Big Rock Cemetery to decorate graves.

After Jim and I married, we made our annual pilgrimage to the cemeteries where our loved ones were buried. Sometimes it was a strain on our budget to buy flowers to decorate the graves, but it brought a sense of peace as we continued the traditions of our youth.

Our first stop was always Mt. Carmel. From there we went to Big Rock Cemetery, stopped at Stover Cemetery, and then drove back to Sedalia to decorate graves at Crown Hill. We made a complete circle and headed home with a heart full of memories.

When Jim first developed dementia, I drove our usual route while Jim placed the flowers on the graves. When Jim went in the nursing home, I went alone. Decorating graves without him was not an experience I cared to repeat.

Memorial Day 2006 was the first time I participated in the ceremony at the Missouri Veterans Cemetery at Higginsville. I haven't missed a year since Jim's death.

I was a little bummed about a conflict this year. My granddaughter is graduating kindergarten Sunday. My youngest son's family lives in the Lake of the Ozarks area, the opposite direction from the cemetery. I told my older son, Eric, that I was going to the graduation. "I'll miss the Memorial Day ceremony," I told him.

I was disappointed, but I know Jim would have never chosen a ceremony for the dead over one for the living. He often wondered aloud what good it did to make someone a hero after they died. Jim always said, "Dying doesn't automatically make you a hero." Instead, he would tell our sons when they were small, "You are my hero."

Jim never considered himself to be a hero. He was tightlipped when it came to Vietnam, and I never knew Jim had received an Army Commendation Medal until he could no longer tell me why he received the award. The commendation was nowhere to be found, and the Army couldn't produce it when I asked.

"Why would you miss the ceremony when the graduation is Sunday and Memorial Day is Monday?" Eric asked.

"I don't know why I thought Memorial Day was Sunday," I said. "After all, it's always been Monday."

On Memorial Day, I'll drive to Higginsville cemetery to place flowers in front of Jim's niche. I'll be there with my sister-in-law, Ginger, and other families to think about and honor our loved ones. When we pause to honor our fallen heroes, we should honor our everyday heroes too. We all know people who face life's challenges with bravery.

I think about how Jim told our sons they were his heroes, and how prophetic his words would become. They truly became his heroes when they cared for him with love and respect as he faded away.

For most people, decorating graves is an afterthought as they travel home from a weekend at the lake. Others spend the weekend shopping at Memorial Day sales or pigging out at backyard barbecues.

I always thought it ironic that Memorial Day has become a party weekend instead of a somber occasion to remember the dead. Maybe it makes more sense to use Memorial Day as a time to celebrate life, and honor the living, as well as our fallen heroes. After all, we are surrounded by everyday heroes who deserve recognition for facing life with courage.

# The Alzheimer's Project
## Sunday, May 31, 2009

When Jim was first diagnosed with dementia of the Alzheimer's type, I knew nothing about the disease. One day shortly after Jim's diagnosis, I watched an HBO special on early-onset Alzheimer's. The show followed a brother and sister with the genetic form of Alzheimer's. The sister was in the end stages, and the brother was beginning to need help dressing himself. I remember the gnawing feeling in the pit of my stomach when his wife fastened his belt. As the sister lay dying, the younger generation, a boy and girl in their teens, talked about their fifty-fifty chance of developing early-onset Alzheimer's. That show was a crash course on the relentless disease and how it affects the entire family.

With families of 5.3 million Americans traveling the Alzheimer's journey, HBO has developed a documentary called *The Alzheimer's Project*. HBO opened their airways to non-subscribers to make this program available to the general public. Anyone with Internet access can watch the programs on the Alzheimer's Association website at http://www.alz.org/.

Many reviews have been written about *The Alzheimer's Project* and this is not going to be one of them. I'm only going to talk about my reaction to the series.

I did well on Part I, "The Memory Loss Tapes," until the death scene. Too many things about that scene brought back the emotional tumult of Jim's death. As I watched the family's faces, I remembered the inner struggle to face the reality of our journey's end.

My first reaction was HBO should not have shown that scene. My friend, Ted, whose wife is in the final stages of the disease called me to make sure I knew about the series. He said, "They are telling it like it is." I had to admit he was correct.

I imagine not everyone at HBO was in agreement about showing the death scene. I had the same internal struggle about including the final story in *Alzheimer's Anthology of Unconditional Love*. I was afraid "The Aftermath" would be too depressing, but something compelled me to share Jim's death and my reaction. Caregivers and people with Alzheimer's have enough to deal with to make it through the day-in-day-out struggle with dementia. Did I want to let them know that the death of their loved one is the final insult? That was the moment I realized that no matter how much I had done, the disease won.

Part II, "Grandpa Do You Know Who I Am" shows how young people see the disease. I think about how my grandchildren never knew what Jim was like before dementia. Their image, like some of the children in the film, is of a different person whose brain has been destroyed by disease.

The "Caregivers" is helpful with its real life experiences, and we plan on showing this film at our support group. Knowledge is power and the more we know about the disease, the better caregivers we are.

Jim developed aphasia early in the disease and wasn't able to tell me what he was thinking or how he felt. I was blessed by becoming friends with people with Alzheimer's who retained their communication skills. I learned so much about how a person with Alzheimer's feels from my friends with the disease. I truly appreciate their insights, fears, and hopes.

"Momentum in Science," both parts, assures me that progress is being made toward diagnosing and understanding Alzheimer's effect on the brain. One of the researchers featured in the film, Randy Bateman, MD, from Washington University, accompanied our Missouri Delegation on legislative visits at the Public Policy Forum in 2008. I was impressed with his down-to-earth manner.

The early HBO series helped me understand Alzheimer's, but *The Alzheimer's Project* has a much wider scope with its marriage of personal stories and the hope of scientific breakthrough. Unless science moves forward and finds a cure for Alzheimer's and related dementias, death is the conclusion of the disease.

I look forward to the day when we have Alzheimer's survivors walk a victory lap at Memory Walk. Until then, the only survivors of Alzheimer's are the caregivers and families.

# Wild Turkey Alarm Clock
## Saturday, June 6, 2009

Living in the country is sometimes a mixed blessing.
The peace and quiet was interrupted this morning by
the loud, obnoxious gobble, gobble, gobble of a wild
turkey who seemed to be outside my bedroom window.
I looked at the clock and thought I could sleep for two
more hours and still be getting up early for a Saturday
morning. The turkey thought differently.

I have to admit that in all the years I've lived in this
house, I've been awakened by barking dogs, cat fights,
thunder, and several other annoying morning noises,
but not once has a turkey been close enough to the
house to gobble me awake.

I knew turkeys lived in the nearby woods. When Jim
was building our house, he was up at the crack of dawn
every day to work on the project. As soon as Jim started
hammering, the turkeys began to gobble.

Missouri is overrun by turkeys. They are awkward in
flight, and seem to make up their minds to fly across the
road just as a car is swooshing by. My sister wound up
with a tom turkey in her lap one time when he crashed
through the windshield.

Turkeys are more pleasant to watch when they strut in
the fields, where they belong. Each morning on my way
to work, I look at the field I think of as a deer and

turkey haven. Deer and turkeys seem to frequent the same type of habitat. Some mornings I'll see five or six deer and a dozen turkeys.

A few weeks ago, I saw an unusual sight. In a misting rain, a friend and I were approaching the toll bridge near Lake Ozark. A turkey crossed the road with about a dozen poults lined up behind her. The traffic stopped while the turkey family meandered across the highway.

All these ruminations about turkeys should have put me back to sleep, but the persistent turkey outside my window gobbled every time I drifted off. I peeked through the blinds expecting to see him in my yard. I'm not sure what I would have done if he had been in my line of vision, but I was seething murderous thoughts.

Finally, I decided to get up and make coffee. While the coffee brewed, I put on a light jacket. I walked to the road and retrieved the paper from the box. On my return trip, I heard wings flopping and saw a huge bird flounder off a limb of the oak tree. He flew ungracefully across the gravel road, barely clearing the fence, and out of sight into the field.

For a moment, I puzzled over what the heck that awkward bird could be. Suddenly, it dawned on me that my turkey alarm clock was going off duty. It never occurred to me that turkeys roosted in trees.

I walked into the house and poured myself a cup of coffee and carried it into the living room. I opened the patio doors to a world of chirping birds and barking squirrels. With my early start on the day, I had plenty of time to relax over coffee and the paper.

Yes, indeed, living in the country is a mixed blessing. I'm up earlier than I planned, but it's shaping up to be a beautiful day.

# Murphy's Week
## Saturday, June 13, 2009

This week has been really long and totally wrong.
Monday was my day off, and I don't have any
complaints about it.

Murphy's Law was in full force beginning Tuesday,
which seemed like a bad Monday to me. I started down
the stairs to take towels out of the dryer. I flipped the
switch and the stairwell light burned out. Why is it that
when one light burns out it starts a chain reaction?
When I turned on my closet light, it went out too. It's
always dangerous for me to choose my outfit for the
day when I can't see into the depths of my closet.

At work I spent the morning putting out fires instead of
working on month end. At noon, I made a trip to Dollar
Tree to buy table decorations for an upcoming meeting.
I was proud of my efficient shopping until I couldn't
find my car keys.

I finally set my packages on the ground and thoroughly
searched each compartment of my new purse. No keys.
I patted down all my pockets, first the raincoat and then
my slacks. My son has a set of keys so I knew (as a last
resort) I could call him. One time when he bailed me
out, he happened to pull on the door and it wasn't
locked. I don't like repeating mistakes so I checked the
car door. It opened, and I fully expected to see my keys

in the ignition. They weren't! Now what? Then, I saw them in the cup holder.

You would have thought that would have been enough excitement for one day. After work, I went to the gym to de-stress, and when I came out I noticed my trunk lid was up. I must have pushed too many buttons when I locked the doors. I walked over and casually closed it like I always leave my trunk open even in a rain shower.

The good thing about Wednesday—it had to be better than Tuesday. I forgot my closet light was out until I flipped the switch and nothing happened. Still, I managed to get dressed and out the door on time. At work, I jumped into month end. I was a woman on a mission: Make up for yesterday when everything seemed to go wrong.

An hour later I wanted a cup of coffee and headed down the hall to the kitchen. I was preoccupied with work, but noticed one shoe was clicking and the other wasn't. I looked at my feet and discovered I had on two black shoes but they definitely weren't mates. One was my Liz Baker shoe with about an inch heel and the other was a Clark shoe with flat rubber soles. And I thought my limp was because of my bad knee!

I pondered what to do about this wardrobe malfunction. My first thought was to sit at my desk and keep my feet out of sight. That didn't seem like such a great idea since I had plans to go to friendship lunch at noon. I couldn't imagine walking into Bandana's with mismatched shoes on my feet.

Following the suck-it-up-and-deal-with-it philosophy, I walked into my boss's office. "I need to go home," I told him. I knew it wouldn't be a problem to go home, but I didn't want to just disappear for half an hour.

"Is something wrong?" he asked. His concern was so touching that I couldn't lie.

"Not really," I said. "I just need to change my shoes. They are both black, but they aren't mates."

On the way home, I thought about how my week had been going. I was beginning to feel pretty silly, but blamed my problems on brain overload. I'm sure it has nothing to do with my impending birthday or that nonsense about senior moments. I saw how dementia changed Jim, and I know the difference.

I decided to go with the Clarks which are the most comfortable shoes I own. As I drove back to work, I decided the burnt-out bulb was the reason I pulled out mismatched shoes. After all, if anything can go wrong, it will. Isn't that the basis of Murphy's Law?

We'll skip the rest of the week including almost running out of gas and pumping it in the middle of a thunderstorm. One great thing about today—the week is winding down to its overdue end. When I wake up in the morning, it will be a brand new week and I can scoff at Murphy's Law.

# He Wouldn't Harm a Fly
## Saturday, June 20, 2009

It must have been a slow news day for the president to create such a whoop-la-la by smacking a pesky fly. Especially when you consider the nasty little creatures carry life threatening diseases on all six of their dirty little feet. Spreading diseases isn't enough for adult flies—they lay their eggs in places where the larvae can burrow into flesh and damage internal organs in unfortunate animals.

I wonder if the PETA guy who protested the president swatting a fly has ever been bitten by a horsefly. Well, I have and they hurt. Although the lowly fly causes pain and suffering for just about every other living animal, PETA is supplying the president with a special trap that will not harm the flies. The idea is to take the trapped flies outside and set them free.

All this concern about small creatures reminds me of an incident that happened when Jim was in the early stages of dementia. We were headed to town in Jim's Nissan pickup. I was driving, and Jim sat beside me. We had just turned onto the blacktop when he began to pull against his seatbelt and leaned forward into his seat.

"No!" he shouted. "You're killing them!"

For some unknown reason a mass of caterpillars were creeping across the blacktop. "No! No!" he shrieked. "You're running over the worms."

"I can't miss them," I said. "They're everywhere."

Jim was really upset about the creepy crawlers, but I just ignored his protests. Why he was so upset, I really don't know. It was just one more glitch in his thinking.

I can honestly say I cannot recall one time that I was deliberately cruel to any animal. I make it a habit to swiftly deal the fatal blow when necessary. Maybe it's just me, but I have a tendency to kill flies, ticks, spiders, or any other critters I find in my house, or on my body. If PETA considers killing annoying, disease-carrying bugs mass murderer, then I plead guilty.

Oh, wait. No one really cares if I kill flies because I am not the President of the United States. Sometimes it pays to be an ordinary person instead of the rich or famous whose every indiscretion is caught by a watchful camera lens and published on YouTube.

I found a tip on the Internet that makes me think PETA may be on to something with that trap. Flies follow each other in their constant hunt for food. If you catch a few flies in the trap, their buzzing will attract more flies. Once the trap is full of flies, you can get rid of them.

Maybe you are the kind who couldn't harm a fly and will set them free. Or you may be a person who plans to terminate those suckers and rid the world of disease carrying pests.

# Home Videos: I Cried Until I Laughed
## Sunday, June 28, 2009

Yesterday, I decided to sort some of our old home
videos. Jim was the cameraman and captured every
vacation and important event on tape. Sometimes, I
would get irritated with him for turning our lives into
reality TV. Usually, I preferred to unpack while he
played the tapes for the family.

While Jim was in the nursing home, I couldn't bear to
watch any of the tapes. By then, he had lost his ability
to carry on a conversation. He was my best friend, and I
missed how we shared our deepest thoughts and
feelings, our hopes and fears. After aphasia stole his
conversation skills, he became more and more silent
and spoke only a few words in repetitious phrases.

Jim had meticulously labeled each tape with his initials,
JDF, and when, where, or what the tape contained. I
picked up a tape labeled: "Colorado 1988" and popped
it into the VCR/DVD player. My screen was filled with
majestic mountain scenery, deer, elk, and coyotes as
Jim taped one of our animal watch evenings in the
Rocky Mountain National Park.

Jim videotaped our campfire breakfast the next
morning, and to keep him from running the video
camera while driving the curvy mountain roads, I taped
our drive through the park. Jim, as usual, narrated. I
turned the camera on Jim and he began to talk about our

plans for the day. "We're having the time of our lives," he said.

Tears welled up as I watched Jim on the video and was reminded of the man he had been before we knew anything about dementia. He spoke in his quick-witted manner, relaxed, and happy in his beloved Colorado. The mountains worked their magic on him giving him an inner happiness and peace that he didn't have in our normal world. I was beginning to think that watching these films was depressing and a really bad idea.

"We're going to the Big Horn Meadow," Jim said. "I'm going to feed the chipmunks." Jim was pretty good to follow all the rules and regulations in the park, but he had always fed the chipmunks.

"Why not? It's only a $25 fine—per offence," I said.

"We can afford $25," he answered.

Jim's bantering from more than twenty years ago chased away my tears, and I found myself laughing out loud. Somehow in my memories, I had forgotten Jim's great sense of humor.

During one of our hikes, Jim had the camera, and he said, "I've dropped back to film because Linda doesn't like for me to film her from behind. Ooops," he said as the camera caught my rear view.

He swung the camera aside and then back, "Ooops. And ooops."

As we drove up Fall River Road next to a sheer drop off, Jim teasingly asked if I wanted him to get closer to my side of the road so I could get a better picture. "Oh, no," I said, "I'm fine."

When the tape came to an end, I popped in a couple of tapes marked "Idaho" to see what they were. At least that's what I told myself. One of them was a trip Jim took to Idaho without me. Jim shot footage of his cousin Joe in Idaho and in the next segment the camera zoomed in for a close-up of a McDonald's sign. "Hey, honey, guess where I am! This is the only McDonald's I ever liked to eat at."

"Estes Park!" I said from my seat on the couch where I still held the remote in my hands.

"Estes Park!" he said…as if I wouldn't immediately know.

There's no danger that I will ever forget Jim as long as I'm breathing, but memories are limited. Most of the moments caught on film were buried so deep within my brain I would probably have never retrieved them. Watching the tapes are a way of reminding me of the wondrous moments I've lived, even if nostalgia makes me cry until happy memories make me laugh.

# Music Therapy Stimulates Memories
## Saturday, July 4, 2009

Music stimulates our memories and unveils feelings we thought we had forgotten. Have you ever noticed how a song can bring back a flood of emotions? A familiar melody can take us back in time, and although our physical appearance might shriek middle-age, our emotional age is the era of the song.

If you don't think music can transform you internally, pay attention to the songs that give you happy feet. Even if your body isn't up to the dance moves of your youth, your heart hears the music and your feet want to dance.

Throughout the years of our marriage, Jim played his guitar nearly every morning. He called it his therapy. At work I often listen to KDRO radio, a local station that plays country music, and almost every song makes me think of Jim. One of the saddest things about dementia was when Jim began to have trouble playing his guitar. One day he asked me to tune his guitar. Jim, the man with perfect pitch, wanted tone-deaf me to attempt something I had never done in my life. I knew his request was beyond my abilities, but I called his brother and he took care of it.

Music has been a family tradition in my mom's family. I grew up thinking that all normal families played guitars and sang. On Saturday nights my mom and her brothers, neighbors, and friends sat on wooden kitchen chairs and played music for hours. On those Saturdays at Grandma and Grandpa Whittle's house, my Aunt Venetia always sang my grandma's favorite gospel songs.

My mom, Aunt Labetta, Jimmy (my brother), cousin Reta, and Gene Branch play music at the nursing home one Saturday a month. Recently, I dropped by Good Shepherd Nursing Home in Versailles to listen to the music. I wound my way through the halls to the dining room where the family band was on the stage. Several residents tapped their toes and sang along with the songs they knew. At the front of the room, my Aunt Venetia sat dozing in her wheelchair while my cousin Jan attended to her.

My mom and Aunt Labetta, as always, dedicated a special song to their sister-in-law. Aunt Venetia is in the late stages of Alzheimer's, yet she perks up when she hears the music she's loved her entire life.

When Jim was in the nursing home, his favorite channel was GAC. His eyes were glued to the set when his favorite entertainers performed. His foot would tap in time to the music that he once effortlessly played.

With the special bond music has to our memories, it is no wonder that eyes sparkle at certain songs. Sometimes the sparkle is caused by unshed tears, but often it's just memories dancing in our brains that bring life to our eyes.

# Thinking with My Heart
## Sunday, July 12, 2009

This week I received email newsletters from two trusted sources, Alzheimer's Weekly and the Alzheimer's Association, about a Swedish/Finnish study. The crux of the study was a marriage, so to speak, between dementia and committed relationships. I perked up when the researchers concluded that widows (like me!) were three times as likely to develop dementia as married women. I read new studies the same way I read a horoscope—I pick out the parts I like and bah-humbug the rest.

The researchers say that social involvement will help offset the dementia risk of living alone. That's good news for me since I am by nature a social being. I have been an Alzheimer's Association volunteer and advocate for the past fourteen years. I'm an officer in a local business women's group. Talk about an active club! We move from one project to the next, and have monthly meetings, weekly friendship luncheons, and several great conferences each year. Last, but certainly not least, I'm president of the Columbia Chapter of the Missouri Writers' Guild. Oh, and did I mention I work full-time as office manager at a rural electric cooperative? So, I think I have "social" covered.

When the Alzheimer's Association first unveiled their Maintain Your Brain program, I had mixed emotions. My friend, Diane, and I were delegates at an assembly meeting in Chicago when we first heard about the program. Diane's husband had recently died from early-onset dementia, and she was concerned people would begin to think dementia was brought on by unhealthy habits. I had to agree with her.

Yes, we all want to do things to keep our minds healthy, but what about people like Jim? He read, played the guitar, knew the lyrics to hundreds of songs, and he was only forty-nine years old. He certainly was not at risk for dementia.

After I learned more about the program, I liked the common sense idea behind the science. Maintain Your Brain can be condensed into a few basic categories: stay mentally, socially, and physically active, and while you're at it, eat brain healthy food. How to develop these simple, but effective, brain healthy habits can be found on the Alzheimer's Association website at

http://www.alz.org/we_can_help_brain_health_maintai n_your_brain.asp.

Heart and brain health are connected in many ways. So think with your heart, but before you sign up for e-harmony.com consider other factors that can reduce your risk of dementia. A good rule to keep in mind is that if it's good for your heart, it's good for your brain.

# Life is Good
## Saturday, July 18, 2009

I found myself in a funk—tired, rundown, and overdrawn on vitality. To regain my normal optimistic outlook on life, I decided to take a mini-vacation with nary a single plan to clutter up my do-nothingness. Usually the idea of taking three days off work in the middle of a Missouri July means chilling out under the air conditioner.

Wednesday, I went to Kansas City and wore a "Life is Good" T-shirt for luck. I ventured into Dick's Sporting Goods to see what kind of mid-summer bargains they might have. I practically glowed with optimism when I found my favorite T-shirts on sale and snapped up four "Life is Good" long-sleeved T-shirts. Well, I figured I couldn't wear them until fall, but knew I'd get my money's worth then.

When I was in Boston last year I visited the original Life is Good store. That's where I heard the Bert and John Jacobs' story. These two guys made their start by selling T-shirts out of the back of a van. With a creative idea and a vanload of optimism, their achievements must have exceeded their wildest optimistic dreams.

Sometimes in my life, it's been hard for me to remain optimistic, but it is in my nature to look for the good in life. That helped me make it through the ten years of Jim's dementia. I sought out the good times, the quiet times, the loving times. I found that by cherishing those small moments of joy, I could make it through the bad times.

As we travel the river of life, we hit snags, whirlpools try to suck us downward, and sometimes we wind up high and dry on a sand bar. When we navigate through dangerous rapids we find ourselves in mortal danger as we cling to life.

We can recognize the dangers of a river, but often don't recognize the risk of stress. Warning signs are everywhere—high blood pressure, chronic fatigue, depression. We need to find a calm, quiet place and mentally regroup. We all need respite from the pressures of life. If we don't take time for ourselves, our inner optimism will die from lack of use.

My mini-vacation became respite from work and hot weather. A friend and I had a backyard barbeque Thursday evening and as we relaxed in lawn chairs a cool breeze sprang up. Who would have thought we would have 70 degree weather on a mid-July evening?

Today, I awoke to 60 degree weather and guess what? I broke out one of my Life is Good shirts. I removed the tag and realized that my shirt is named "Acoustic Jake."

I still find joy in life's small treasures. I find comfort in reading inspirational books like Joel Osteen's *Your Best Life Now* and *Become a Better You*. This morning, my uplifting reading came from a tag off my Life is Good shirt. These words surround the logo on the tag: "Do what you like. Like what you do. Optimism can take you anywhere."

Life *is* good.

# Living Words: Therapeutic Writing for Early-Stage Dementia
## Saturday, July 25, 2009

Lauren Holland, a student at Wofford College, came across my "Writing as Therapy" blog post and sent an email two weeks ago about the Living Words program. I answered her email and casually goggled Wofford College to see where it was located. My Goggle search informed me that Wofford is in Spartanburg, SC.

That information made me smile because that's where my good friend, Ralph Winn, lives. I met Ralph at the 2001 Alzheimer's Association Public Policy Forum in Washington, DC. Ralph and I, both board members at our local associations, were attending the forum with our respective executive directors. We hit it off at the executive directors' reception.

"Oh, you are a board member, too," Ralph said with a charming southern accent that immediately made me realize he was indeed a southern gentleman. "I guess we are crashing this party," he said. Ralph figured he might be distinguished as the oldest participant at the meeting, but he was determined to be an advocate for his lovely wife who had Alzheimer's.

The next morning I was free to explore Washington, DC, while my executive director was in a meeting. I called the front desk and asked to be connected to Ralph's room to ask him to go with me. He wasn't in his room, so I decided he might be people watching. Sure enough, I found him sitting in a big comfy chair in the lobby. That day we toured the Smithsonian and our friendship was born.

Today, I received a second email from Lauren in Spartanburg, SC. This time Lauren mentioned their website, and I decided to visit the site to learn more about the Living Words program. This therapeutic writing workshop is for individuals with dementia and a caregiver or friend who accompanies them. I read blog entries, sample stories, program descriptions, and followed a link to a newspaper article about a father and daughter reconnecting because of the program.

I know from personal experience that writing is cathartic and have always recommended it as a way to cope with stress and grief. I knew from stories submitted by Tracy Mobley and Charles Schneider to *Alzheimer's Anthology of Unconditional Love* that writing helped my friends with dementia. Tracy tells me writing helps her express herself better than speaking. Writing gives her more time to think about what she wants to say. Writing is not easy for her, but it is well worth the effort.

The Living Words website chronicles the writing program in sufficient detail to allow implementation of this program in other communities. The website serves as a template for support groups, facilities, or other organizations to help families touched by Alzheimer's benefit from writing.

Participants are not pushed into writing, but gently nudged into exploring their memories or stretching themselves to creatively answer writing prompts. Workshops are conducted with humor and encourage camaraderie between caregivers and their loved ones with dementia as they share their ideas, thoughts, and reminiscences with each other. Living Words is a concept with the potential to use the therapeutic benefits of writing to improve quality of life for families living with Alzheimer's.

Visit Living Words website at www.livingwordsprogram.com and see if you can be inspired to offer a similar program in your community.

# Compassionate Allowances
## Monday, August 3, 2009

On July 29, the Social Security Administration held a hearing on the need for Compassionate Allowances for individuals with younger-onset Alzheimer's. Harry Johns, president and CEO of the Alzheimer's Association, was among the experts who testified for the need to streamline the application process for Social Security Disability.

By including younger-onset Alzheimer's and related disorders on the list, the waiting period for benefits will be greatly reduced. In his testimony, Johns said, "Through the Compassionate Allowances process, Social Security can avoid the extra costs to the agency of numerous appeals and families can avoid the financial and emotional toll of going through a long decision process."

I was interested in the testimony about primary progressive aphasia. Although many people are aware of Alzheimer's, including early onset, they are not aware of lesser known related disorders. When I read the testimony of Darby Morhardt, LCSW, in support of primary progressive aphasia, I was surprised to find that Frontotemporal Dementia (FTD) was placed on the Compassionate Allowances list in 2008, but not Alzheimer's disease and related disorders.

Considering the difficulty of diagnosing which particular type of dementia a younger person may have, I don't understand how FTD can be on the list and not Alzheimer's and related disorders. Placing FTD on the list was a proper move, but that addition in itself speaks to recognition of the devastating financial and healthcare problems caused by dementia when individuals are too young to qualify for regular social security.

If younger-onset Alzheimer's and the lesser known related disorders are added to the list of Compassionate Allowances, it would speed up the Social Security process for this group who falls between the cracks.

When Jim was diagnosed with dementia of the Alzheimer's type, his attorney told us it could hurt his Social Security Disability claim. We had gone through countless appeals for disability based on Jim's loss of motion and constant pain in his neck and shoulder. We were in the final appeals process when Jim began to lose his ability to communicate. His aphasia made it impossible for him to present a coherent testimony at his own disability hearing. Our attorney asked us to wait in the hallway while he presented the successful appeal to the judge. We had been in the appeals process so long that Jim received back pay and retroactive Medicare.

The very nature of dementia impedes the disability process. Jim was one of the lucky ones. Not lucky in receiving his Social Security in a timely manner. He was lucky because I had a job with health insurance.

What happens to those with younger-onset dementia who get stalled in the process because they cannot speak for themselves? How does a family survive when a person with Alzheimer's cannot work and requires constant care?

Too many times a person with younger-onset dementia loses his job before diagnosis. Often a loss of employment means the end of health insurance. Without a job and the inability to get a new job, it is impossible to afford COBRA. It can easily take two years to get a diagnosis of early-onset dementia and even longer to receive a favorable disability determination.

When a person of any age is diagnosed with Alzheimer's or related dementia, it places the entire family under emotional stress and financial strain. To include younger-onset Alzheimer's type of dementia on the Compassionate Allowances list would relieve families of one of the frustrating worries following diagnosis.

Source: http://www.alz.org/

# Hurry Up Patience!
## Saturday, August 8, 2009

On this hot August Saturday morning, I grabbed a cup of coffee and hopped onto the Internet to check email before making my weekly blog post. "Hopped" may be too bold a word to describe dial-up in a high-speed world. My computer looks like the one on the right in the commercial—the one that has loaded a sliver of data while the one on the left displays a complete picture.

My first introduction to a computer was in 1980 when I was hired to enter customer information on an IBM System 34. I typed data onto a screen, pressed enter, and waited a half minute or so for the information to be added to the file and display the next input screen. It all seemed pretty fast compared to the handwritten sheets we filled out in the subscription department of *Full Cry* magazine.

My home dial-up has become a virtual turtle in comparison to the high-speed Internet at work. To make matters more inequitable, this week our IT department installed a new Dell computer with two gigantic side-by-side screens. Now I can open up a dozen programs and slide displays around until I can see them all. It makes me feel like an interior decorator. Does my calendar look better here, or here? Oh, heck, I'll just slide it on across to a different screen.

On my dial-up, I find myself gritting my teeth while I wait for a graphic laden website to load. I remind myself that patience is a virtue, but why can't it just hurry up?

I'm torn between wanting speediness and longing for a more relaxed lifestyle. This Saturday morning is so different from the days I spent, lying in bed drinking coffee with Jim, waking up slowly, and not being rushed to do anything. The two of us would fix breakfast and sit at our kitchen table laughing and making plans.

Of course, as dementia changed the entire fabric of our lives, mornings sometimes started with Jim pouring water into the pot without a carafe to catch the coffee. Or I might wake up and find him missing, jump in the car and drive down the road looking for him. Relaxation changed to stress, and I discovered that for a person without patience, I learned to accept our life's changes remarkably well. The "Serenity Prayer" became more than a plaque on my wall.

I was never able to revert to my days of leisurely plans and now have a mental to-do list that nags me constantly. Sometimes, I have to re-enforce my memory with a written list, an electronic reminder, and sticky notes plastered to everything. I need beeps, bells, and visual aids to keep me moving forward. All I need to figure out now is how to multitask multitasking.

I became a blogger on Well*sphere* this week and Well*sphere* encourages members to set goals and share those goals with like-minded people. So far, I haven't set any. My goals are planted in my head and can keep me awake at night with small encouragement. Doesn't a goal of a more laid-back lifestyle seem counterintuitive?

My brother-in-law, Terry, calls people who are constantly on the go "busybodies." I find his meaning to be more fitting that the traditional definition of the word. I've become a busybody, and don't have time to be patient. Heaven help me, I have a high-speed mind in a dial-up body!

****

Check out my Profile and Blog on Well*sphere*!
http://www.wellsphere.com/l-s-fisher-profile/143451

# Country Living—Not Just for Farmers
## Sunday, August 16, 2009

The State Fair started Thursday with a parade and $1 night. By the time I got off work at six o'clock, we had already heard that traffic was snarled and you couldn't get close to the parade route. Without giving it a second thought, I headed north toward home avoiding the whole mess, fair and all.

Our fair always has a theme, and this year the theme is "Rural Lifestyles Showcase" with an emphasis on "Country Living—Not Just for Farmers." I'm not sure which is really the theme, but it would seem that the Children's Barnyard beat out the carnival for top billing this year.

The State Fair changes everything in Sedalia and puts a crimp in our rural lifestyle for the duration. Getting across town usually takes about fifteen minutes on a high traffic day, but during the fair, traffic jams up from one end of town to the other. We have two kinds of locals—those who spend a lot of time at the fair, and those who leave town.

I've lived in Sedalia since 1972, and I've seen a lot of fairs come and go. I have fond memories of Tammy Wynette singing to Jim, a lot of great concerts, free shows at the Bud tent, herding kids through the carnival, corndogs, ice cream and snow cones.

The last time Jim went to the fair, his dementia had advanced to the point he needed to be supervised. I had asked Jim if he wanted to go to the Clint Black concert with me and he emphatically declined my invitation. I made arrangements for my niece, Rhonda, to go with me instead.

At the last minute, Jim changed his mind. When I couldn't get a seat anywhere near ours, I bought two tickets and asked his sister, Ginger, to take him.

It was quite an adventure for Ginger to try to keep up with Jim. She had to be pretty quick to pay for the water he pulled out of the barrels in front of the vendor carts.

After a busy afternoon and evening at the concert, we walked to the parking lot together. Rhonda and I pulled out, while Ginger and Jim sat in his Nissan truck. I figured they would be along soon. When they finally got home, Ginger told me she turned the lights on, but each time she let go of the knob, they went off. Jim laughed at her, but couldn't tell her how to get them to stay on. They sat in the lot until Ginger finally figured it out.

Yes, I have fond memories of the fair, but I also remember sunburns, blistered feet, sick kids, lightening and wind storms, and suffocating heat. A few years ago, I took my grandkids to the fair and if they hadn't helped me find the car, I might still be wandering around the parking lot looking for it. Last year, I found my car after the Air Supply concert, but in the unlit parking lot, I drove around looking for a way out that didn't involve a deep ditch. I finally followed another car out of the lot that seemed to know how to find the lone driveway. It almost makes me think I shouldn't be attending the fair without supervision, at least after dark.

I plan on working a few hours at the Rural Electric Co-op Building this year. That will probably be my one and only time at the country showcase. Other than that, I plan on avoiding town until the fair is over and our rural lifestyle returns.

# Not So Friendly Competition
## Saturday, August 22, 2009

This year at the fair, I controlled the energy bicycle. Dawn, one of my co-workers, gave me a quick demonstration when I took over for her.

"Flip on the fan first," Dawn said. "Anyone can get that going." The idea was to peddle the bicycle to generate enough energy to light up a series of items. "I do the florescent light next, because it's easy too."

I gave it a try. I got the fan going and the florescent light flickered feebly. Then, the bike felt like it hit a brick wall—and I was done.

I felt like a Carney beckoning people to step up and test their skill. Most people could start the fan, a lamp, a teensy TV, and the florescent bulb, but when I switched on the 25 watt bulb, the game was over. Another loser! Five bulbs remained unlit.

My boss dropped by the Co-op Building and hopped on the bike to show what he could do. He pumped away without showing any exertion—ah, to have the energy of the young again. I flipped switches working my way from bottom to top. He began to breathe harder and with only two switches left he couldn't budge the pedals.

About an hour later a teenager wanted to ride the bike. Her mom signed the permission slip, and the teen hopped on. She peddled, and I flipped switches. Her face turned red, but she kept on pumping. She stopped at the same level as my boss.

"You're tied for first," I told her. Her mom immediately signed a slip for herself and tied the daughter. Not to be outdone, Dad straddled the bike. He peddled until his face was beet red, but he slightly edged out his daughter and wife by making the last light burn brighter. I really hoped he wasn't going to have a heart attack on my watch.

"You must be a competitive family," I remarked to the mother at their not-so-friendly competition.

"Oh, yes, we definitely are!" she said.

"I understand," I said. "I come from a competitive family too."

Could that be an understatement? I thought Jim and I were going to come to blows a few times over cards. He and Aunt Nita were the most infuriating pitch players I ever saw in my life. Uncle Johnny and I couldn't seem to beat them very often. They bid like lunatics. "I'll bid eight, on my partner's hand," Jim would say. Then he would toss a small card out, but if I put a point on it, Aunt Nita would throw a bigger card on. The next thing you knew, she would dominate the round with all the big trumps.

When Jim developed dementia, he became confused about which cards to play. His mom helped him. He was competitive enough to bid. From the look on his mom's face, I knew he was still bidding his partner's hand. From experience, I knew it would work most of the time.

Jim was always competitive with his Uncle Vic and Uncle Orvie. They played checkers at a furious level. The bet was the checkerboard itself. The loser had to sign away his championship and give the board to the winner. Uncle Vic had possession of the checkerboard when he died unexpectedly. He left the checkerboard and the championship to Jim.

Jim and Uncle Orvie were Mario Kart aficionados. Uncle Orvie's rheumatoid arthritis twisted his fingers into odd shapes. You would think Jim would have cut his uncle some slack due to his handicap. No way. Those two played game after game. "Let's go for the best two out of three," the loser would say. "Now let's play for the championship—the best nine out of ten!" On and on they played. Each wanting to win the fierce, not-always-friendly competition.

In "You're Going the Wrong Way" published in *A Cup of Comfort for Families Touched by Alzheimer's* I describe my dismal Mario Kart experience. I not only couldn't beat Jim, I couldn't keep my kart on the track going in the correct direction.

"I don't know how to play," I would tell Jim after I lost another game. "Which buttons do I push?"

His aphasia had limited his communication skills and he couldn't explain the game to me. "I have no idea," he would say, using one of his stock phrases.

Right before he zipped Toad across the finish line, he would remind me, "You're going the wrong way!"

He would tell me how to play if he could, I always reassured myself. Surely that was not the gleam of not-so-friendly competition in his eyes. Or was it?

# Vacation—Recharging Batteries
## Saturday, August 29, 2009

Colorado mountain pines whisper my name and beckon me to the quiet hush of a cool mountain morning. I always referred to vacation as a time to recharge my batteries, but it doesn't have quite the same meaning it used to have.

I fell in love with the mountains on our first camping trip in 1983. To humor Jim, I agreed to camp at the Moraine Park campgrounds in Rocky Mountain National Park. Everyone expected us to be home after a few days because, to put it mildly, I never considered camping to be a relaxing experience. Sleeping on a hard surface in extreme Missouri heat, while slapping mosquitoes, was not my idea of fun.

Jim was an accomplished camper from a lifetime of outdoors adventures. He loved the Colorado mountains and each year we set aside a week to get away from everyday stress and recharge our spiritual batteries.

Jim spoiled me on our vacations. On cool Colorado mornings, he would rise before the sun peeked over the mountains, build a campfire, and brew coffee. Jim would open the van door, and hand me a cup of coffee while I huddled under the heavy quilts in bed.

"Breakfast is almost ready, Princess," Jim would say. The scent of bacon frying on the Coleman camp stove promised a tasty, hearty meal. "Get up sleepyhead, we are in the mountains!" Joy would shine on Jim's face as we planned the day—an aerial tramway ride, hiking, and an early evening drive through the park to watch deer and elk.

In retrospect, I can measure the progression of Jim's dementia by our trips to Colorado. By 1997, camping was beyond Jim's capabilities and although we still drove to our beloved mountains, we stayed in a hotel. Then, the trips ended as Jim became more confused and eventually entered long-term care.

After Jim's death in 2005, I made a bittersweet return to the mountains. Long's Peak looked the same, but I noticed other changes. We used to walk around the Beaver Pond to watch ducks and fish in the clear water below. Now, a small trickle moves past a truncated ramp near the reclaimed meadow. A drive up the Big Thompson doesn't seem as great without browsing the Glen Comfort store filled with exquisite Native American pottery and storytellers.

Now, instead of camping at Moraine Park, I find a hotel with high speed Internet. The batteries I recharge are in my Dell netbook, camera, and cell phone. Instead of getting away from it all, I take it all with me.

Maybe it's my age, but I find some of the changes to be good. I can idealize past vacations through selective memory, but a lot is to be said for having a private bathroom, satellite TV, air conditioning or heat as needed and a comfortable bed. The cell phone and Internet keep me from getting behind on everything happening back home. Now, I can take hundreds of pictures on my camera and never have to buy a roll of film.

Yes, many things have changed, but vacation shouldn't be an attempt to recapture the past. It should be a time for new experiences, to breathe the fresh air of today and appreciate the beauty of now. When I look at the majestic view from Trail Ridge Road or gaze at the reflection of the mountains in Bear Lake, I feel a small charge of electric current flow through my spiritual self. Can that be my batteries recharging?

# Ted and Norma: Promises to Keep
## Tuesday, September 1, 2009

On October 3, Ted Distler and his lovely wife, Norma, will celebrate fifty years of marriage. I admire Ted for his devotion to Norma and how he has held her hand and guided her through the quagmire of early-onset Alzheimer's.

Besides being a devoted husband, Ted honors Norma by being a tireless volunteer for the Alzheimer's Association Mid-Missouri Chapter. We met in 1999 when Ted was at the helm of the Jefferson City Memory Walk and I coordinated the Sedalia Memory Walk.

Ted was a formidable fundraiser, and I made a valiant effort to stay in the competition. Although we squared off like championship boxers, we were cheerleaders for each other as we joined forces for a common cause. Our ultimate goal was to help support families facing Alzheimer's and a cure for their loved ones, and our loved ones. We knew our local Chapter was providing that support for Mid-Missouri families.

Ted and I met for coffee one day and worked on a story for *Alzheimer's Anthology of Unconditional Love*. Norma and Ted's story of unconditional love, courage, and devotion is posted on the Mid-Missouri Chapter's website at http://www.alz.org/mid-missouri/in_my_community_17573.asp.

Congratulations, Ted and Norma! I wish you blessings and love with each step of your journey.

Ted and Norma's Story, "Promises to Keep," is published in *Alzheimer's Anthology of Unconditional Love*.

# If I Make it through September!
## Saturday, September 5, 2009

My life has turned into a NASCAR speedway and sometimes I feel like I'm driving a tricycle. It leaves me in danger of being pancaked by the big boys.

I'm not sure how it got to be September already. What happened to summer? Please don't tell me I Rip Van Winkled right past it. Considering my sleep deprivation, that doesn't seem logical.

Somehow I survived the summer without once shinnying into a swimsuit, visiting a beach, suffering heat stroke at Silver Dollar City (so much for season tickets!) or for that matter, turning lobster-red from a sunburn. What a waste of summer months, and uh-huh-oh summer nights.

I thought Halloween was supposed to be scary, but it doesn't come close to the feeling I had in the pit of my stomach when I flipped the calendar page and saw all the scribble marks. Here I am on Labor Day weekend, laboring, trying to catch up to all the events that are now staring me in the face.

Today started with a radio program "Open Mike" where Chris and I talked about Alzheimer's and our September 19 Memory Walk. Then, I stopped off at the office to use high speed Internet and my duo screens to send emails and media releases for two different organizations. After four hours, I had made a small dent in my calendar to-do list.

I only have fourteen "events" written on my calendar, so shouldn't that mean I have more free time than scheduled time? That might be true if they were events where I just had to show up, but it doesn't work that way for those of us on the planning committee or in charge. Oh, and let's not forget the 101 items that didn't make the official calendar. That would be those things I intend to do if I have time.

One of the best things about hectic life is I never have time to be bored, or even think about being bored. My goal on Well*sphere* is to take thirty-minute stress breaks five times a week. That doesn't seem like too lofty a goal until I actually went through the stress of trying to find a spare thirty minutes.

In the meantime, I'll just keep peddling until I make it through September, and then, I can relax awhile. After all, I have two free weekends in October. Yes, if I make it through September, I'll be fine.

# White Rabbit Syndrome: Always Late
## Monday, September 14, 2009

 My daddy used to have a saying, "A day late and a dollar short." It was not a good thing to be the person he referred to when he pulled his brows down in a frown and uttered the words. He had many pet peeves and being late and not paying lawful debts were near the top of the list.

I'm not sure what has happened to me over the years because I struggle with being on time. I wasn't raised that way. I've self-diagnosed a bad case of White Rabbit Syndrome. People with this rare disorder rush all the time only to catch every red light in town, have to wait on the longest freight train in history, spend hours searching for car keys, or have to turn around and return home to turn off the coffee pot. Clocks and watches are not their friends.

The world has just now begun to recognize this disease, and a conspiracy is already afoot to release White Rabbit Syndrome suffers' names to email spammers. My evidence is the large number of "cheap luxury watch" offers I receive in my inbox each day.

Does anyone in his right mind buy a watch from an unsolicited email? They seem to be wising up to my lack of interest in their watches because now I can't open an "Important Information" or "Important Request" without finding another watch offer.

I was explaining this to my son, Eric, a few nights ago as we chowed down on Long John Silver's fish and chips.

"I get a lot of email from my website and blog," I told him. "I hate to just delete mail from names I don't recognize just to keep from looking at more watch offers."

"Speaking of watches," my daughter-in-law the nurse said, "did you ever get an offer for one with military time, and numbers with a second hand? At work I have to use military time, but I need a second hand too."

"I bet I'll be offered that kind of watch," I said. "Oh, guess what I found? My old Timex! I think it was still ticking."

I bit into a hushpuppy. "Do you remember how you kids used to want to go to Long John Silvers so you could get a pirate hat?"

"Yeah, I always liked to eat there when I was a kid," Eric said.

I don't remember feeling so rushed back then. I also remember getting to work before anyone else. I always seemed to get a lot of work done in the quiet hours before all those tardy last-minute-peel-into-the-parking-lot workers arrived. I scoffed at how they jumped out of their cars and raced for the time clock.

I was younger then, too. Another one of my dad's
sayings when one of us kids didn't jump fast enough,
"Grandma is slow, but she's old."

Funny how those words keep popping into my head
lately. I'm a grandma, so maybe I'm entitled to slow
down a bit. I don't admit to being old though. If I were
old, I'd just rest my case on my daddy's words and
White Rabbit Syndrome.

Instead of another watch offer, someone needs to offer
me a time machine. If I could make time speed up, slow
down, or move backwards at will, I might be on to
something. Then, I could just go back and do "overs" as
Jim always called it. Unfortunately, we don't get the
opportunity to do overs—time wasted is time gone. Just
like my Timex, time keeps on ticking until it's going,
going, gone.

# The Friendship Connection
## Sunday, September 20, 2009

When Whitney and her friend Mariah donned their balloon hat, it reminded me of how we are connected to our friends. Don the Balloon man's hat-for-two gave the friends a different kind of connection at our Sedalia Memory Walk this year.

Friendship connections have evolved since my friend Sharon and I wrote notes in study hall. To keep our words private, we wrote them backwards and held them up to a mirror to read them. Now people email, text, Twitter, or use Facebook. Many of us have cell phones with nationwide plans and think nothing of calling someone across country to chat for a few minutes.

Not too long ago, I was riding with my daughter-in-law and my grandkids were texting each other—and they were both in the backseat. Of course, one advantage of text messaging is that siblings can have a disagreement without getting the parents involved.

I finally caved to the pressure and opened a Facebook account. It is a good way to stay updated on what is going on in my friends' lives. I'm sure all friends on Facebook are not necessarily friends in the true sense of the word. Many of these "friends" are only casual acquaintances. A person is not a friend unless we care about what happens to them, we keep their confidences, and we overlook their faults. We support our friends and celebrate their successes without a twinge of envy.

When we meet people, we feel an immediate connection with some but not others. Our friends aren't necessarily mirror images of ourselves. Sometimes we are drawn to others because they have a trait or skill we lack but admire.

I have been blessed with many friends. My involvement in my business women's group, writers' guild, work, and the Alzheimer's Association brings me into contact with a lot of talented people. A combined effort to support a cause forges a lot of other personal differences to create a bond.

The Memory Walk took months of planning, organization, leg work and fortitude. My sister-in-law, Ginger Dollinger, and team coordinator, Sheila Ream, logged countless hours of preparation. All this effort birthed a fun Memory Walk with music, balloons, face painting, raffles, prizes, and a cake walk.

Friends pitch in and help you when you need it. That's what Connie Pope did when she saw we needed help at Memory Walk. Cindy stopped to visit while I signed books, casually bagged them and handed them out with a smile. Brenda called to let me know she couldn't be at the walk because she felt she needed to stay with her gravely ill husband. Sheila gave me a comforting hug as we released our balloons at the end of the walk. These are just a few of the contacts I made with friends at one event.

My favorite part of Memory Walk is spending a few hours with family and friends—hugs, smiles, and a lifting of spirits as we connect with each other. Weeks, months, and years disappear when I greet a friend after a separation.

We don't need a balloon hat to physically connect us to our friends. A real friendship connection is not diminished by miles and time. It has no boundaries or limits and lives deep within our hearts.

# Put My House in Order
## Monday, September 28, 2009

For the past week I've been trying to put my house in order for our annual family reunion. This year I'm the hostess for my seven siblings and their families.

My busy life has turned home into the place where I sleep, and housekeeping has fallen by the wayside. While putting my house in order, I've sorted through years of paperwork and dug into hidey-holes. I've stayed up past my bedtime every night for a week while I sorted, dusted, tossed, or packed items in plastic storage tubs.

If I had been on a scavenger hunt, I would surely be a winner. I found the USB for the MP3 Player I recently replaced with an iPod. It was still an ah-hah moment to discovered I had tucked it into an old camera case. In my Suzy Homemaker mode, dusting wasn't good enough so I removed a cloth angel for a thorough cleaning and uncovered Jim's long-lost dog tags on the hook behind it. Memories were tucked away in an old Christmas tin. I found tattered valentines from Jim and my eyes blurred when I read his "Love you always" signature.

This week has turned into a trail of discovery as I ferreted out long-forgotten secrets. I am not sure at what point in life I turned into a packrat. It wasn't so bad when Jim was here to coerce me into tossing souvenirs and freebies from conventions and state fairs. On my own, I just tuck them away, and add to the clutter.

While I was frantically cleaning, my co-worker and friend, Brenda spent precious moments with her husband before he left his worldly home and passed to the next. Ray had battled cancer and knowing his time was limited, he worked at putting his house in order. He made his own arrangements and wrote his obituary. His family knew his wishes and fulfilled them precisely. Following Ray's instructions, his ashes were placed into his Honeymooner's cookie jar. You can almost hear Ray's hearty laugh anticipating the look on unsuspecting faces when they see the "urn" he has chosen.

When friends or loved ones die, it makes us pause and contemplate our own mortality. I often say my kids are going to be really mad at me when they have to sort through my worldly possessions. Barring a horrific accident, I should have time to go through all those tubs filled with things I can't part with yet. I certainly plan to get my house in order so my family doesn't have to rummage through my belongings to separate treasures from junk.

Death also makes me question the order of my spiritual house which has become cluttered and needs a good dusting. Hopefully, when my time comes, my house will be in order from top to bottom, and I won't have to try to make it right at the last minute.

The best thing about a clean house is being able to relax without the mental nagging to get busy and finish. When that day comes, I can truthfully say, "I can rest now—my work here is done." For now, I'm not even close.

# Autumn: Trick or Treat
## Monday, October 5, 2009

How I feel about autumn reflects how I feel about life. When I think of autumn, I think of colorful leaves, pumpkin pie, apple turnovers, Halloween and Thanksgiving. At one time in my life I dreaded autumn's dreary cold days and the miserable weather ahead.

Autumn reminds me of trick-or-treat. Being an optimist, I remember the treats more than the tricks. I lived in the country where neighbors were few and far between so we went to town to trick-or-treat. Each Halloween night it wasn't long before word on the street led us to the houses handing out homemade cookies or popcorn balls. We also learned which house to avoid. That would be where the cranky old man yelled at kids to "Get outta here before I start shootin'!"

One Halloween, Jim and I had the opportunity to play a trick on our boys. They walked up the road to my brother-in-law's house to retrieve our dog who had strayed off looking for romance. The full moon provided their only light. Oh, yes, it was the perfect Halloween night. The wind pushed mysterious clouds across the sky and wispy shadows hinted of witches, bats, or werewolves. Jim and I hid in the bushes near the dirt road. Our two sons were talking to each other or they would have heard our giggles. When they got close, we jumped out screaming and yelling. They were only startled for a moment, and it didn't seem quite as funny to them as it did to us.

Autumn is more than dressing up in costumes and eating candy until we are sick. Our unique inner clocks determine whether the autumn of our lives becomes trick or treat. To some people, retirement means they have lost the focus of their days and feelings of self worth. I look forward to it as a time to spread my wings and fly toward the fulfillment of youthful dreams put on hold for the greater part of my adulthood. I see the autumn of my life as an opportunity to spend time with my grandchildren, write the novel bouncing around in my head, and relax with a good book from time to time.

The autumn of life can be the perfect season to feel young again, a time to taste sweet wine and enjoy heady smells of spice, the scents of fall. Autumn is the time to join in fall festivities and rejoice at the end of harvest—years of hard work and sacrifice.

Chronic diseases like Alzheimer's or cancer have an autumn in their duration. During the autumn of the disease, it is time to decide whether to spend your days dreading the cold winter ahead, or savor the kaleidoscope of burnt orange, warm golden hues, and cheerful yellows. Do you want to taste the crisp juicy apples of fresh harvest, or put them aside and rue the day they became bruised and shriven?

As we sit at the table of autumn fest, our mindset determines how much we savor the bounty on our plates. It isn't so much life's physical tricks—aching backs, arthritic joints, a slow numbing of our minds—as it is attitude and ability to enjoy today for what it brings. When we feel the sun on our faces, it helps offset the cold wind blowing at our backs.

We cannot change the seasons, we can only change how we feel about them. Life should never be in a holding pattern waiting for a season to change. Living life in dread of the next season, and what it may bring, can steal our joy. I believe joy delayed is joy lost. The important thing is to embrace today and celebrate the festivals of the current season. It is our choice whether life is trick or treat.

# Auto Tool Kit: AAA and a Cell Phone
## Saturday, October 10, 2009

One of the first things I learned as a caregiver was that I had to take on new responsibilities. Jim was always the mechanic in the family, and until he developed dementia, I had never changed the oil or listened for strange noises cars make from time to time.

We usually drove old clunkers and never left home without Jim's tool kit. One time our van broke down on a country road, and Jim fixed it with a piece of wire he snipped from a sagging fence. He had us up and running in no time. On another trip, in the dead of winter, our heater began to blow cold air and Jim fixed it with a piece of cardboard. Whatever happened, he analyzed the problem and had an immediate solution.

Jim began to lose his mechanical skills, and we purchased AAA roadside assistance. I missed Jim's expert attention to our vehicles, but with AAA and a cell phone, I figured we had the tools to get by. Besides, the card was good for discounts on hotel rooms, air fares, and even at Hard Rock Café.

Eric, our oldest son, worked at a dealership and reminded me when I needed an oil change or tires rotated. When I had mechanical problems, my first call was to Eric, not AAA.

One time Eric was on vacation and my youngest son, Rob, met me at the nursing home to take Jim out to lunch. We had already loaded Jim into the van before we noticed a tire was flat.

Rob crawled under the van and struggled to release the itty-bitty spare from its holder. After changing the tire, he climbed back into the van covered with sweat and dirt.

I said, "I don't know what I would have done if you hadn't been with me." Then after I thought for a minute, I added, "I guess I would have called Triple-A."

"I just changed a tire in hundred degree weather and you have Triple-A?" Rob asked.

"Yeah, but I've never used it except for discounts," I said. Since 1997 the card had not once been used it for its primary purpose.

My Oldsmobile Alero is getting a little age on it, but overall, it has been a reliable car. That's why I was caught off guard Thursday night. It had been raining all day, and in the back of my mind I was worried that my roads might be flooded.

Still, I went to dinner at Country Kitchen with other members of our Alzheimer's Support Group. After dinner, we popped open our umbrellas and headed for our cars. I was ready to go home where it was warm and dry.

I put my key in the ignition and turned it. Instead of the purr of my motor, I heard dead silence.

"My car won't start," I told David, a member of our group who was parked next to me. He looked under the hood and said the battery connections were good.

I looked at my watch and knew it was too late to call Eric. He gets up so early for work that he would be in bed by now.

"Do you have any kind of road hazard?" David asked. Funny, I hadn't thought about that.

David shined a flashlight on my AAA card so I could dial the number. Within ten minutes, my car was started and back on the road.

Of course, the car wouldn't start the next morning. I phoned a friend who came over and jump started the car for me.

Now that I have a new battery, my car starts when I turn the key. That's the way I like it. But if all else fails, I have my tool kit—a cell phone and AAA. Better yet, I have friends' numbers programmed into my cell phone.

I can't break the habit of calling family or friends for advice about all things mechanical, or to give me an occasional jump start. It's still nice to know I have three Aces in the hole to use for discounts, or in case my friends become wise to me and don't answer their phones.

# In Touch with the Season: Scary Reading
## Saturday, October 17, 2009

In celebration of the impending Halloween season, I decided to read something really scary, so I pulled out my prescription fact sheets. My insurance provider refers to the full page, single-spaced, ten-point font sheet as "Participant Counseling."

The older I get, the more drugs I have added to my arsenal. My health insurance company strongly encourages annual health screenings. Because of this annual testing, it has been easy for my doctor to following my escalating numbers. I'll admit he has been cautious about prescribing maintenance drugs for my accumulating conditions. The preferred line of action was to lose weight, but it seems like I lose the same five pounds over and over.

One of my prescriptions has side effects of dizziness, headache, nausea, gas, stomach upset/pain, diarrhea and constipation (not at the same time, I hope).Those are the minor side effects. My participant counseling sheet for my cholesterol drug has a large section under "caution" which tells me I might have muscle pain or muscle damage which could lead to kidney damage and "a very serious condition" rhabdocmyolysis. I don't know what that is, but I betcha I don't want it.

Another interesting part of the sheet counsels me to not take the medication if I am allergic to any of the ingredients in the product. I am not a chemist and most of the "ingredients" don't look like anything I've ever knowingly taken.

Lately I've noticed television commercials for prescription drugs show active people playing tennis, bike riding, or participating in other activities that make me tired just to watch. The voice over extols the benefits of a prescription for about the first quarter of the commercial. For the remainder of the commercial, a predictable pattern has emerged. A rapid fire voice describes the side-effects and in a slower, soothing tone finishes up with "ask your physician if (fill in the blank) is right for you." Did I hear something about "sudden death" in that quick disclaimer? It makes me wonder how important a prescription is if it's supposed to make you happy, healthy and active, but "oh, by the way" it might cause stroke, cardiac arrest, or liver failure.

One night I was taking my medication and my six-year-old granddaughter asked, "What do those pills do, Grandma Linda?"

I looked at the handful of pills and started pointing to each one. "This one is for my cholesterol, this one for high blood pressure, this is a vitamin, this is for my knee pain," pointing to a half of a Tylenol PM, I said, "and this one is to help me sleep."

"Oh, and look," she said, "it is two colors—blue to help you get to sleep fast and white to help you stay asleep."

Her comment shows which part of the commercial sticks with us the best. After all, I'm sure no drug company would advertise if we weren't more impressed with the benefits of medication than we are with the downside.

With his dementia, Jim took a lot of medication. Through the trial-and-error to find the best drug regimen for him, I diligently read the side effects of everything he took. He was no longer capable of reading them, and I felt responsible for looking out for his wellbeing. Once I mentioned to the doctor that a new drug Jim was taking had a side effect of confusion. The doctor told me that all medicines have potential side effects. That doesn't mean that everyone has them. He pointed out that no one would take prescription drugs if we worried too much about side effects.

It's not just prescriptions that have unexpected side effects and warnings. All over-the-counter medication has them too. That night-time cold formula "so you can rest" medicine cautions you to quit taking it if you suffer from "sleeplessness." On non-drowsy cold capsules, one of the first side effects mentioned is drowsiness. That certainly won't help your job performance if you take it to help control your runny nose during the day.

One good thing about it, Halloween will soon be over and we will be moving into the Thanksgiving and Christmas season. There's nothing scary about those holidays and my reading needs to reflect that. I'll put away the prescription fact sheets and dig out some inspirational holiday reading instead. I'll stick with the delightful and forget the frightful.

# In a Perfect World
## Sunday, October 25, 2009

I've been pushing myself a lot lately and can't find enough hours in the day to get everything done. This morning I basked in a few rare hours of downtime and watched ice skating on TV. Ladies figure skating has long been my favorite sport, and I can't help but be amazed at the discipline and talent that goes into each performance. Part of my admiration stems from an inability to even walk on ice. A few years ago my feet swooshed out from under me causing me to fall flat on my back and crack my head on a surface as hard as concrete.

Many years ago I talked Jim into taking me to St. Louis to see Stars on Ice. At the time, Jim was in the early stages and we were hopeful his problems were caused by something treatable like depression or a vitamin deficiency.

The trip went smoothly except when Jim drove the wrong way on a one-way street. That could happen to anyone in the confusing downtown area of St. Louis.

We checked into a hotel overlooking the river and within sight of the Arch. Our room was nice, but the bed had only two pillows, exactly Jim's requirement. He called the front desk and said, "My wife doesn't have a pillow." It was obvious he had claimed both pillows and decided I didn't have any.

The next year we went to Stars on Ice in Kansas City. As we approached Kemper Arena we were directed into a small parking lot tucked between tall buildings. We couldn't see the arena because of the buildings crowding all sides of the lot but found it by following the crowd headed to the show.

The very air feels different at a live skating show. On TV it's easy to be critical when the performance isn't perfect. At a live performance, the amazing talent of professional skaters shines in a different light. A death spiral seems much scarier in person. The man spins at great speed, swinging his partner around and around, up and down, until you shut your eyes because it looks like he will surely slam her head into the ice. You see the "air" beneath the jumps and wonder how a human can develop such skill. Yes, to be at a live ice skating event, you realize that a great skater may not always skate perfectly.

We were still hyped from the show when we exited the building. We realized we had no idea where our car was parked. Jim had always had a great sense of direction and I depended on him. The January night was frigid and the crowd thinned as everyone hurried to their cars. My stomach hurt when I realized it was going to be up to me to figure out where we were parked.

"We need to go to the other side of the arena," I told Jim. We walked around Kemper and saw a sidewalk headed toward some buildings. "It has to be down this way, don't you think?"

"I have no idea," Jim said. Boy, were we ever in trouble.

"I know it's this way," I said with more confidence than I felt. We walked toward the dimly lighted buildings. After a few blocks on the deserted sidewalk we veered down a dark alley. Our car was the only vehicle left in the lot.

It's been years since I've watched a live skating show and found this morning's televised skating performances disappointing. The skaters fell, popped jumps, or made two-footed landings.

Then, I thought about the pressure on today's skaters. Skaters must execute perfect triple or quadruple jumps to be competitive. A champion skater cannot remain in a comfort zone, but must take risks. As a result, skaters make multiple mistakes or miscalculations. When I remember Scott Hamilton executing a perfect back flip, it is unimportant if he fell from time to time or popped a jump.

In a perfect world we wouldn't falter or fall. But it isn't a perfect world and we are only human. If we never stretch ourselves, we may not fail, but we won't know the joy of living our dreams. We can stay in our

comfort zone and settle for mediocrity, or take a risk
and push ourselves to the limit.

# Fall Back: An Extra Hour
## Saturday, October 31, 2009

Don't you just wish they (whoever they are) would leave the time alone? Since I get up so early, I prefer standard time. Psychologically speaking the lighter the sky when I leave for work, the more awake I feel.

The best thing about the time change is the extra hour we have between Saturday night and Sunday morning. Have you ever thought about how much difference an hour can make? For some reason I can't stop thinking about it. An hour can be the difference between life and death.

If I had not been in the exact place at the exact time I would not have met Jim on that summer Saturday in 1968. An hour would have changed my entire life and the lives of my children and grandchildren.

It's easy to fritter away an hour here and an hour there. Most of the time an hour is insignificant, but at other times it can come at a high price. When you miss a deadline by one measly hour, you can lose your job. If you don't spend an hour studying for a test, you could fail a class. If a flight is delayed one hour, you can miss a connecting flight, which can cause you to miss an important meeting. An hour can be the difference between owning a home and seeing it reduced to smoldering ashes.

145

An hour can seem like an eternity if a loved one is missing. When Jim wandered off, minutes seemed like hours while we searched for him. The locale was different, but the heart-stopping fear was the same whether he was on our own road, lost in an airport, wandering around the mall, or lost in a crowd at Silver Dollar City. An hour can be the difference between a safe return and a tragic outcome.

Some surgeries only take an hour. I had an obstinate gallbladder removed in an hour. That hour meant living my life without painful attacks.

An hour can be for good or for evil. It can make a life changing difference or be of no consequence at all. When you think back over the last week, can you recall one single hour in detail? Can you think of an hour you would take back and erase if you could?

Those of us with fulltime jobs work 2080 hours per year. Our work day sometimes seems to be made up of slow moving hours. Of course, we need to deduct vacation and holidays. When we are involved in a hobby or favorite activity, an hour speeds past on amazingly fleet feet.

Our lives are made up of hours. Those hours meld into weeks, months, years and become a lifetime. In the final hour, we learn the true meaninglessness of time.

We gain our hour tonight while most of us are in bed asleep. An extra hour can be the difference between being well rested or suffering sleep deprivation. It can be the difference between a dream and a nightmare.

But tonight, the time changes and we gain an hour. Have you thought about how to spend that precious extra hour? I don't know what you plan to do with that bonus hour, but I plan to be sleeping. Soundly. Dreaming sweet dreams. Banking the hour for next spring when they (whoever they are) take it away and we lose an hour.

# Turtles, Tunnels, and Denial
## Saturday, November 7, 2009

Turtles, our slow-natured friends, are the beneficiaries of a government sponsored windfall. Plans are afoot to provide a $3 million tunnel for Florida turtles to allow safe passage beneath the busy highway.

We wouldn't want turtles to be hit by cars and become unwilling missiles. Does the so-called expert that says this happens think turtles are a top-secret weapon of mass destruction?

I will admit that living in rural Missouri, I've run over my share of turtles. I've seen others meet with a sad fate while simply trying to cross a country road or state highway.

I hate to hit a turtle. I've never seen one become a missile, but I've certainly heard the sickening "plop" as the shell crunches. It makes me feel bad to know I've unwittingly killed a living creature. Sometimes, I'm lucky and straddle the little slowpokes and spare their lives. Other times, we are both unlucky.

Jim created his own turtle/terrapin crossings. When he spotted one of the little fellows in the road, he stopped the car, got out, and carried the docile creature across the road. Hopefully, he saved as many lives as I took with my carelessness.

One day my son had hitched a ride home from school with one of his buddies. They saw a turtle in the road, and Eric told his friend that his dad helped them across the road so they wouldn't get hit by a car. Eric's friend was so inspired by the story, he pulled over and jumped out of his vehicle. As he reached for the turtle, instead of hiding in his shell, the turtle viciously snapped at the hand that was trying to save him. All turtles are not created equal in the humble department and the Good Samaritan has the scars to prove it.

Just think how long the crossing takes when the turtle stops and pulls in all appendages and sits there all snug inside his shell thinking he is safe. Instead of the shell providing a safe haven, it just means he is in harm's way longer.

It's easy for us to see that the turtle is in denial of the danger lurking around the next corner. We understand denial because it is an all too human emotion.

I heard a story of denial at lunch yesterday. A group of us attended a luncheon prior to an educational program about the genetic studies being done on Alzheimer's disease. I sat next to a nurse who provides counseling for families dealing with Alzheimer's. She mentioned her own denial when her mother first displayed symptoms of dementia. Logically, she knew her mother's behavior couldn't be explained away, but emotionally, she grasped at hope born from denial.

When you are in denial, you are inside the shell with the turtle. It makes the world feel safer, but it can put you and your loved one in harm's way. While you are in denial, a family member with dementia may continue to drive when they shouldn't. You may leave for a few hours and return to an empty house because your loved one has wandered. Your denial makes you a turtle in the middle of the road with a speeding car fast approaching.

Wouldn't we like to keep our loved ones safe? I'm sure that if $3 million would keep our families safe, we would be willing to pay it if we had it. The key word is *if*. A certain faction of our society thinks no amount of money is too much to keep the world safe for small critters, but don't worry about how the money is being taken away from our fellow humans. How much safer could the highway be made with $3 million? How many human lives could be saved with the money used to "protect" turtles?

The problem is turtles cannot be kept safe by a tunnel. Perhaps the turtles will be safe while they are in the tunnel, but the big, dangerous world exists on both sides. No amount of taxpayer's money will keep the turtles safe. No living creature lives in a vacuum and no tunnel could be big enough or long enough to protect life except for a fleeting moment.

# Hugs Are Better Than Drugs
## Friday, November 13, 2009

In the past few weeks, I've had the opportunity to attend some outstanding Alzheimer's training. I also read two good books about dementia.

In late October, I went to the Alzheimer's Association Heart of America's *Train the Trainer, Building Creative Caregivers.* Last Friday I went to the Mid-Missouri Chapter's program on genetic studies. No matter how much I learn about Alzheimer's, I pick up new information at each program I attend and from each book I read.

At the *Building Creative Caregivers* training session, I received a thick workbook. As I began to read through the details of all the modules, I came across reference to *The Best Friends Approach to Alzheimer's Care* by Virginia Bell and David Troxel. The book goes hand in hand with the "Person First" module in the *Train the Trainer* manual.

I sat on my porch this afternoon reading the book. I found "An Alzheimer's Disease Bill of Rights" to be a logical set of guidelines. In the detail, for "To be free from psychotropic drugs, if possible" I saw the statement: Hugs are usually better than drugs. I wholeheartedly agree with that statement.

*The Best Friends Approach* is written with professional caregivers in mind. It is a way to provide care based on meeting psychological as well as physical needs of a person who has been diagnosed with dementia. Family caregivers know the history and preferences of their loved one, but when professionals treat everyone the same, they are denying our individual natures and preferences.

It is important to minister to the soul and spirit as well as physical needs when a person faces the challenges of dementia. Bell and Troxel liken Alzheimer's disease to a long trip in a foreign land where we can't speak the language, know the customs, or understand how to use the phone.

When caring for a person with dementia we must concentrate on what they can do rather than what they cannot do. Can they still enjoy a walk? A drive? A cup of coffee where they can watch birds gather at a feeder?

Jim was a musician and never lost his love of country music. He had a personal tape player with headphones. When the tape ended, Jim had to rely on someone else to turn the tape and play the other side. How easy would it be now to fill an iPod with someone's favorite music?

At the Mid-Missouri program this week, one of the staff members asked me if I had read *Still Alice*. She told me she had just finished the book and thought it was excellent. I bought the book from Lisa Genova last March at the Alzheimer's Association Public Policy Forum. I had heard a lot about the book, but when I realized Genova based the fictional story on her research of early onset Alzheimer's rather than personal experience, I figured it was another glamorized story about Alzheimer's with no basis on reality.

I read *Still Alice* in a few days. Genova makes Alice seem like a real person and you can feel Alice's confusion and grief as the disease brings an end to her familiar life. The journey for Alice and her family are realistic. The conflicts between love and loss, selfishness and generosity, denial and acceptance have been experienced by millions of families when they realized their loved one could not be cured.

Yes, the past few weeks have been filled with learning. Last night at support group, we showed "Momentum in Science Part I" from *The Alzheimer's Project*. Although I had watched the film before, I learned from it. It was interesting to see the relationship between brain disease and overall health.

Much has been learned about Alzheimer's disease, but so much remains a mystery. As scientists seek effective treatment, we must provide the best care possible for those who have the disease now.

With a best friend's approach, we can provide person first care to improve quality of life whether a person lives at home or in a long-term care facility.

Hugs are indeed better than drugs and a lot less expensive.

# Everything Changes
## Monday, November 23, 2009

Last weekend evolved into a whirlwind of shows and shopping. A girls' weekend—friends spending time together in Branson.

Visiting Branson and Silver Dollar City is a metamorphic experience for a native Missourian. Our little moth has changed into a glitzy butterfly, and the razzle-dazzle masks the charm of small town Branson.

When I was a student at Hard Work U, Branson had a four-way stop and two or three small country music theatres. Dick's Five and Dime was there, but instead of being a tourist attraction, it was just a place where you could buy inexpensive items.

Silver Dollar City has changed from a small local attraction with a train ride, the Fire in the Hole and a few pickers and grinners to an extravaganza of professional shows, thrill rides, lights in every tree, bush, hollow, building, structure, and a five-story Christmas tree—four million lights in all.

Branson is always bittersweet for me because Jim and I spent a lot of time there, especially after his dementia made our trips to Colorado much harder. Being a musician himself, Jim loved the music shows. His favorite performer was Tom Brumley and the highlight of each Branson trip. We had season passes to Silver

Dollar City and enjoyed taking our grandson with us when he was little. I'll never forget the weekend when he and Jim went into the restroom, and I waited and worried about what was taking them so long. While I vigilantly guarded the door, they walked up behind me. They had exited on the other side of the building and my four-year-old grandson led his grandpa back to me.

I have more memories of Silver Dollar City and Branson than they have Christmas lights. This weekend, I added to those memories. The production of *A Dickens' Christmas Carol* was performed by a talented troupe that would have done Broadway proud. As if that wasn't enough, my friends and I experienced Cathy Rigby as *Peter Pan*. The show had so much magic that we all went home with pockets full of fairy dust and determination to never grow up.

Branson and Silver Dollar City have both become unrecognizable—different, but still hold the magic of a lifetime of memories. Where my dad used to fish is now a multi-million dollar shopping area known as The Landing. Streetscaping with gaslights, fountains, Christmas lights, old fashioned trolleys and street performers give it the look and feel of other upscale "old town" shopping centers scattered throughout the United States.

I'm sure a lot of tourists feel like they've taken a step back in time when they visit Branson. Sometimes I feel like I've leapt into the future and don't really know this place at all. Branson is like a rock star with countless facelifts to deliberately remove the flaws and accidentally erase the character that made it unique.

The hills don't look anything like they did forty years ago, but then neither do I. Everything changes. How we react to those changes determine whether we continue to enjoy life or groan about the "good ole days." I don't know about you, but I intend to find as much joy as I can while I pass through this world.

Branson is most definitely filled with entertainment choices and great places to eat. Even with my determination to be flexible, I'll admit that slow moving traffic, elbow to elbow shopping, and trolling for a parking space is annoying. Spending time with friends and enjoying world class entertainment adds to my treasure trove of happy memories.

# Let it Glow
## Saturday, November 28, 2009

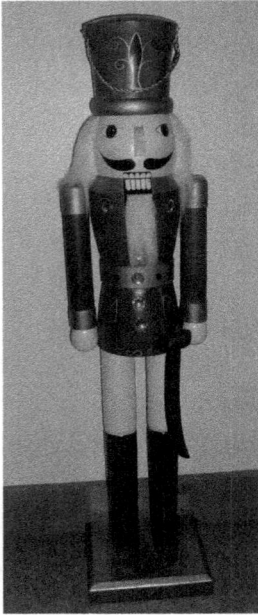

Black Friday is theoretically the biggest shopping day of the year, but I did my share of helping the economy during my Branson trip. Friday, I slept late and spent the day leisurely dragging out my Christmas decorations. I usually start with my Old World Santas, but this year began with the nutcrackers instead. With careful arrangement, most of the nutcrackers fit on the shelf above my entertainment center.

It was a beautiful day and ideal weather to string the lights on the back deck. Last year, the day of our family get-together, a friend and I wound the lights around the railing wearing gloves and heavy coats.

Once the tree was up and the fiber-optic bear lit, it was time to relax with a spot of tea and flip the switch for the lights. I'm still a far cry from the Griswolds, but this as glowing as lights get around my house.

It's not like me to decorate for Christmas this early, but for some reason, I was compelled to begin on Black Friday. I've enjoyed a leisurely vacation this week staying close to home. I worked on my manuscript, but didn't push it too much and opted for some much needed downtime.

Several years ago, we de-stressed Christmas by changing our tradition. When we have our family gathering, each adult brings an inexpensive gift to exchange. I buy educational CDs for my grandchildren and a few small gifts.

When I was unloading the Christmas totes yesterday, it was bittersweet. I found the tiny Christmas tree I used to put in Jim's room at the nursing home. I came across a framed snapshot I always set out during the holidays. It is a picture of Jim, me and our oldest grandson sitting on the living room floor in front of the Christmas tree. Jim is wearing his denim jacket, Vietnam Veteran's cap, and dark sunglasses. The picture is not dated, but this outfit was his hallmark of early dementia.

Pictures freeze a small moment in time. Can I remember what I was thinking at the moment the camera snapped? Maybe not, but the look we share is filled with love and happiness.

One year, when I put photographs in a box to clear the shelves for decorations, Jim took them out of the box and set them back on the shelf. He didn't want me to change things, he wanted familiar family pictures.

This will be my fifth Christmas without Jim. Christmas is probably the hardest holiday for people who have lost a loved one. From childhood we build high expectations of what Christmas should be and are disappointed when it doesn't reach the level we anticipated. Once we understand that the greatest gifts are not wrapped in shiny paper and topped with bows, we are free to celebrate the real gifts in life.

This year, I look forward to the holiday season with an inner peace and joyfulness I haven't felt for a long time. My joy has nothing to do with shopping, buying or receiving presents. It has to do with family and friends, to love and be loved.

A picture perfect Christmas needs snow and glistening trees. One Christmas refrain is, "Let it snow!" A heart perfect Christmas needs love and hope. When I flip the switch and the house is aglow with Christmas lights, my expectation is that the brightest glow will be in my heart and on my face.

Here's to wishing your holiday refrain will be, "Let it glow!"

# Widows Don't Wear Black
## Sunday, December 6, 2009

Tuesday was my first day at work after a week's vacation. When I opened my mail, I saw an advertisement that Senator Jean Carnahan would be at Sedalia Book and Toy to sign *The Tide Always Comes Back*. I had met her during my annual pilgrimages to Washington, DC, for the Alzheimer's Association.

On the drive to the bookstore, I scolded myself for giving in to temptation. Hadn't I spent several hours cataloging more than 250 books in my home library the day before? Didn't dozens of unread books sit on my shelves? No amount of mental chastisement kept me from being one of the first people in line to buy the former Missouri senator's book.

Jean became an accidental senator when her husband was elected to that office posthumously. Taking office so soon after her husband's death in a plane crash, Jean jumped into the challenge of representing her state and didn't dwell on widowhood. In *The Tide Always Comes Back* she wrote: "Sure, I've checked those marital status boxes on printed forms, but I have never thought of myself as a widow in the traditional sense. For so long, society has identified widows as poor, sniveling souls unable to face the world."

I read this passage to Brenda, a co-worker who was recently widowed. "I just filled out a form at the doctor's office and wondered why they needed to know that I was a widow. I almost didn't mark the box," she said.

The average widow is fifty-five years old and remains a widow for fourteen years. Each year, 700,000 women are widowed. At one time widowhood was a way of life, but modern women do not wear black for a year and enter into a dignified state of mourning. The truth is most widows are back on the job shortly after the funeral. We see strong women reel, fall to their knees, and then bounce back at astonishing speed.

Many people read my blog and do not realize I am a widow. I interject stories about Jim and caregiving so that others may benefit from our experiences. When I think of widows, I remember Jim's reaction after his Aunt Mary, and then his mother, were widowed. "I think widows are secret gadabouts," he said. His theory was reinforced when my mother was widowed a few months later.

Not long ago, my mom and Aunt Labetta dropped by work to visit me. Aunt Labetta put her arms on our shoulders and said, "Here we are—three widows." It's strange to think of myself as a widow, and it's not easy to identify either of those two active, laughing women as widows. They travel, occasionally make a run to the casino, and play guitars together.

I don't know any traditional widows. The widows I know are resilient and unafraid of life. Often, death of a loved one reinforces the importance of living life to the fullest. Marriage that lasts until "death do us part" leaves a sense of fulfillment.

The years Jim and I spent together will always be a major part of me. The give and take of marriage, the ups and downs, and Jim's devastating dementia have shaped my personality and endowed me with a life's mission. I do not write about Jim and the life of a caregiver due to unrelenting grief. Writing about life helps me heal and gives me hope that my future is full of adventure, excitement, accomplishment, and love.

The traditional widow is a stereotype. Like Senator Carnahan, I do not think of myself as a widow. I think of myself as a woman who was fortunate enough to have enjoyed enduring love, suffered great loss, and rebounded to a full rich life.

# Alzheimer's Support Group: HBO Screening
## Sunday, December 13, 2009

We watched "Momentum in Science Part II" at our last support group meeting. When a new person entered the room and introduced herself, she said, "My dad is in the film." She didn't know if he was in the segment we were going to watch. I sat close to her and ask her to let us know if he was in this segment. Toward the end, she said, "That's my dad."

I had watched the entire *Alzheimer's Project* before, but picked up more information from the second viewing. An interesting chapter in this part was the DeMoe family story. Six siblings are being studied to try to learn more about familial early-onset Alzheimer's. Out of the six, only Karla does not have the gene that will cause the type of Alzheimer's that ended their father's life at age 58. My heart ached for the five with the disease, but the saddest person was Karla. She has taken on responsibility for her brothers and sisters and already misses them as they spiral into the Alzheimer's abyss.

Researchers believe they can find more effective treatments and possibly an immunization. The immunization trial was put on hold after some of those studied developed encephalitis. Immunization showed promise. It did a marvelous job of removing plaque, one of the hallmarks of Alzheimer's.

When we think about diseases that have been eradicated by immunization, it would seem this would be the best case scenario for Alzheimer's. It would certainly mean a life-changing difference for families like the DeMoe's who have a new generation with a 50/50 chance of developing Alzheimer's.

Dementia is devastating for the entire family. Karla is as much a victim of Alzheimer's as her siblings. She is more aware of their personality erosion than they are. Her siblings will make peace with the disease, but Karla has already begun to grieve their losses.

Each person with dementia is an individual whose life has been decimated. The effects of Alzheimer's types of dementia explodes outward with the power of a bomb blast and attempts to destroy the lives of those closest to ground zero.

My life was forever changed with Jim's dementia. And as heart wrenching as Jim's disease was for me, I think about the DeMoes and my friend Karen Henley whose husband Mike has familial Alzheimer's. Karen's life has been forever changed by her husband's illness, and she must carry a burden in her heart for the possibility that her children may not be safe from the same disease. How much lighter would her burden be if an immunization could protect her children?

During discussion following the screening, we talked about some of the people who had taken part in experimental treatments. The immunization study consisted of giving several small doses of the drug. In the film, a woman whose husband received the injections said, "People kept asking how he was, and we would say he is holding." Holding is about as good as it gets with Alzheimer's. The couple was disappointed and angry when the treatment ended.

Jim was on an experimental drug. I asked my sons for their opinion before enrolling Jim in the Phase III trial. My youngest son said, "Dad would be the first person to want to try it." Jim was on the drug several months, but it had too many side effects and was never approved.

"My dad has changed so much since the film was made," our guest at support group said. "He is frailer now." I knew what she meant. Over the ten years Jim had the disease, his physical appearance changed dramatically.

Families like the DeMoes and Henleys are in the minority. Most people do not know the reality of living with dementia until it strikes their family. Jim was the first and, thankfully so far, the only person in his family to develop the rare form of dementia he had.

According to the film, Alzheimer's is the second most dreaded disease after cancer. More than five million Americans have Alzheimer's and the number of cases is expected to double every twenty years. Researchers are exploring many promising avenues, and work diligently toward changing Alzheimer's from a hopeless disease to a manageable one.

\*\*\*

For information about drug trials or to become an Alzheimer's advocate visit www.alz.org.

# Sparkle Bright with Fairy Dust
## Sunday, December 20, 2009

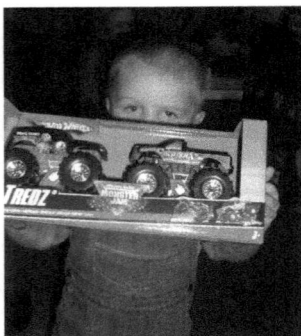

If I hadn't been so busy the week leading up to our family get-together, I would have been better prepared. I spent my day off this week writing articles about Alzheimer's, so my "to-do" list turned into the "didn't-get-done" list.

Saturday, I woke up at 6:30 with the idea of getting an early start. My philosophy turned into what gets done is done, and what doesn't just will not happen this year. While I jumpstarted myself with coffee, my daughter-in-law made biscuits and gravy for breakfast.

My granddaughter stayed with me while the rest of the family went to town. I wrapped presents behind closed doors and handed her gifts to place beneath the tree. I vacuumed and worked on laundry. My granddaughter helped me fold clothes, sort through paper plates, and bring up more decorations from the basement.

 "Grandma Linda, you sure have a lot of stuff down here," she said. She read from labels on plastic storage boxes, "Here's Thanksgiving, St. Patrick's Day, and more Christmas."

The day flew by, but when the rest of the family arrived everything was ready. My youngest granddaughter was Santa's helper and distributed gifts. My four grandchildren range in age from 2 to 15, and have a variety of interests. The older two prefer doing their own shopping so it made more sense to give them pre-paid credit cards. Santa's helper prefers Barbie dolls and princesses. My youngest grandson likes trucks and cars.

In the midst of tearing Christmas paper and prying gifts out of the packaging, shiny pieces of foil flew from the *Peter Pan* book and sprinkled the carpet. "Ooops! Glitter is all over the floor!" my niece said.

"That's not glitter, that's fairy dust," I replied. "Cathy Rigby put it inside the book when she signed it."

Cameras flashed as we captured moments—revving up Monster Trucks to jump Matchbox cars and assembling the Barbie TV Cooking Show set. It's hard to believe that Barbie can cook in those high heels and wearing that mini skirt.

After we—I mean the kids—played with their toys for a while, everyone began to gather up paper, boxes, and debris scattered throughout the house. A heroic attempt was made to scoop up the fairy dust, but it was everywhere so I volunteered to vacuum later.

Considering the chaos yesterday, everything is remarkably back in order. I have a lot of leftovers, but microwaved biscuits and gravy hit the spot.

After church this morning, I switched on the fiber-optic tree, put my feet up and read the paper. I haven't vacuumed yet, and fairy dust winks at me from the carpet. Yesterday my house was filled with love and laughter. Today is silent, peaceful, and a time to reflect on all the magic that has graced my life.

With family time behind me, Christmas seems to be over. The bright sparkle of fairy dust and the lighted tree remind me that Christmas isn't just a "holiday season"—it's a way of life.

# Wrap It Up
## Sunday, December 27, 2009

There has to be a scientific explanation why time goes by faster as we grow older. Maybe we just gain momentum and pick up speed as we race through life.

Another year is almost gone, and we individually and collectively reflect on it. TV tributes abound for famous people who died this year: Michael, Farrah, Bea, Eunice, Ted, Walter, Soupy… Everyone that touches our lives becomes part of us. Sometimes we take celebrity deaths personally, but grief over a superstar is only a fraction of what we feel when something happens to loved ones in our inner circle.

When I was a primary caregiver, the days felt like they had too many waking hours and not nearly enough sleeping hours. Yet, I wanted to grab time and slow it down. Time was the enemy during Jim's slow, steady decline into the land of dementia.

Like it or not, our world changes every day. My son told me a few nights ago that I should get a texting plan for my cell phone. I do something really weird with my cell phone—I talk on it. I believe a conspiracy is afoot to force me to get with the program. I haven't had this much pressure since the kids were embarrassed about the dial telephone hanging on the kitchen wall.

My phone has been out since Christmas day, but I have my cell phone to keep me from feeling cut off from the world. I don't have Internet because I'm on dialup. I can live without checking my email, commenting on Facebook, or even posting to my blog. It's an inconvenience, but I'm not losing any sleep over it.

Our changing world has made us dependent on the World Wide Web. How did people find destinations before GPS systems or Google Map? It is eerie to plug in an address and see images of your house on the screen. Well, they haven't mapped out here in the boonies where I live, but my son's house is not only pictured, you can see their mower kicking up grass clippings. You can become a little figure and walk through the neighborhood.

My granddaughter was playing with Goggle Map and found herself in Hawaii. "Can you find Fort DeRussy Chapel?" I asked. We walked through the surrounding neighborhood, and I saw a lot of familiar landmarks—including the Ilikai where Jim and I spent our honeymoon.

Maybe we should all just become virtual tourists. Think of how much stress, strain, time, and money we could save. I get emails daily about upcoming net meetings. People work from home, and come Monday, I'm going to be mighty jealous of them.

Embracing change and moving forward is the secret to a happy and productive life. We can't live in the past, but the past lives in us.

We each produce, direct, and star in our own reality show. We faithfully tune in each day to experience the next installment. Life, like any good show builds on the previous episodes making the plot more intricate. Characters worm their way into our lives, and we love them just as they are. Once we accept their flaws, we find them endearing.

When we wrap up the past, we open endless possibilities for an unfolding future where adventure waits to happen. In life, we can't fast forward through the bad parts or play the good times in slow motion. We should grasp each moment, and live it to the fullest.

I don't know about you, but I'm looking forward to the New Year just as eagerly as ever. I hope your reality is filled with health, happiness, and love.

# Alzheimer's Anthology of Unconditional Love

## By L. S. Fisher

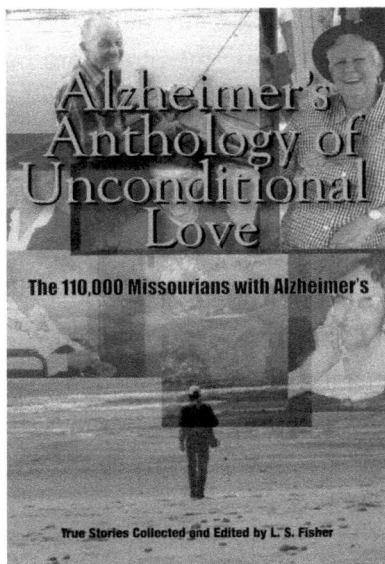

www.lsfisher.com

# Early Onset Blog: Essays from an Online Journal

## By L. S. Fisher

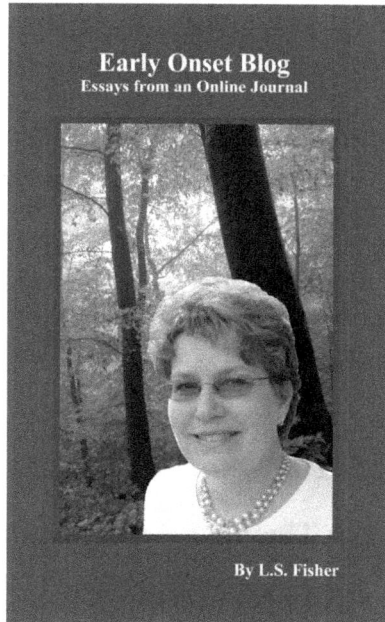

www.lsfisher.com

| Memory Talk | Linda Fisher<br>Alzheimer's Speaker |
| --- | --- |

## Author and Editor
## of
## *Alzheimer's Anthology of Unconditional Love*

Linda is a longtime Alzheimer's Association volunteer and advocate. She speaks from her personal experience as a primary caregiver for her husband who lived with early onset dementia for ten years. She will speak to your group or organization about Alzheimer's or writing life stories. Choose from the following presentations, or request a different Alzheimer's or writing topic:

---

### Writing as Therapy: Rocks and Pebbles

Where are your real life stories? Learn how to reconnect with the pebbles of your life and how writing these stories can be therapeutic. Discover slice-of-life moments that only you know. Suitable for senior adult writing groups, caregivers, and support groups.

**Alzheimer's Voices of Experience**

Learn about Alzheimer's from short excerpts of the heartfelt stories collected in *Alzheimer's Anthology of Unconditional Love*. These true stories allow you to glimpse the lives of real people who have embarked upon an unwilling journey into the world of dementia. This presentation gives a face and voice to the statistics of a baffling disease. Suitable for nursing home staff, caregivers, Alzheimer's staff and volunteers, civic organizations, and people who want to know more about dementia.

---

**Alzheimer's Can Happen at Any Age**

A PowerPoint presentation that focuses on raising awareness that Alzheimer's is a neurological brain disease and not a normal part of aging. Suitable for nursing home staff, caregivers, Alzheimer's staff and volunteers, civic organizations, and people who want to know more about dementia.

---

**Alzheimer's Caregivers: Survive and Thrive**

A workshop to develop caregiver coping skills. Linda speaks from her personal experience as a primary caregiver for her husband who lived with early onset dementia for ten years. Suitable for caregivers.

## Alzheimer's Caregiver Stress

A PowerPoint presentation covering signs of stress and stress management techniques. Linda learned coping skills from her personal experience as a primary caregiver for her husband. Suitable for caregivers and support groups.

---

## Alzheimer's Communication: Hear their Voices

A presentation to develop communication skills. Linda draws on her experience as the primary caregiver for her husband and his difficulty communicating due to aphasia. Suitable for nursing home staff, caregivers, volunteers, and civic organizations.

**To schedule a presentation:**

Email: lfisher@lsfisher.com

## From the Author

My therapist is on call twenty-four hours a day. Some of my most successful sessions occur in the middle of the night when I'm comfortable in my pajamas. I grab a pen and paper or fire up my laptop and write through my worries, hurt, or anger.

I began journaling when I was twelve years old, and knew that writing helped me collect my thoughts and look at my problems more objectively. After I married and began to raise a family, I put away my journals except for an occasional travel log.

When my husband Jim developed dementia at forty-nine, I felt the need to write again. Through the ten years of Jim's dementia, I kept a detailed journal, mostly on tape. When I later transcribed the tapes, I re-discovered a wealth of information to help me heal.

Just like talking to a therapist, writing eased me through the emotionally draining decade of Jim's illness. The power of the pen healed my spirit.

Gathering and editing stories for *Alzheimer's Anthology of Unconditional Love* gave me purpose after Jim's death. I'm still working on a memoir and hope these stories can help others along their journeys.

My love of writing complements my volunteer work and helps me focus on the power of positive thinking and action.

**L. S. Fisher** lives, works, and writes in Sedalia, MO. The greatest tragedy in her life led to her greatest accomplishments. If her husband had not developed dementia, she would spend her days working and her evenings at home. Instead, she has been recognized locally, statewide, and nationally for her Alzheimer's Association volunteer work.

She has just completed *Rocks and Pebbles*, a book on therapeutic writing.

Website: www.lsfisher.com
Blog: http://earlyonset.blogspot.com

Essay originally published in *Bylines 2010 Writer's Desk Calendar*, Snowflake Press, www.bylinescalendar.com

www.ingramcontent.com/pod-product-compliance
Lightning Source LLC
Chambersburg PA
CBHW060242050426
42448CB00009B/1553